You don't have to be a p[...] [...]n to get
*great enjoyment fr*om jo[...] [...]ple are
saying about "T[he New...] [...]river's
"BEST [JOKE BOOK EVER]".

I know a lot of fantastic musicians who are great joke
tellers. I will definitely join the ranks of the best of them with
the help of this book, where every joke is a winner!
- **Georg Wadenius**
Guitarist, *Saturday Night Live, Steely Dan*

I'm having a lot of fun telling jokes from Jim's "BEST
JOKE BOOK EVER" on Elvis Duran's morning radio show.
I loved the introduction to the book that tells how his joke
world began. Then the laughs just keep coming because
every page in this book is fabulously funny!
- **Johnny Pool "Uncle Johnny"**
Radio Personality

I am thoroughly enjoying reading this book. I read 10 pages
every night before going to bed -- sleeping better!
- **Howard Geltzer**
Former Chairman, *Geltzer & Co. Public Relations*
Adjunct Professor, *NYU Stern School of Business*

I've collected jokes my whole life, but only the good ones.
Pietsch goes further: he's collected only the best. There are
jokes in here that are so funny your pet will laugh! In the
world of telling jokes, this book is state-of-the-art, cutting
edge, and slam-dunk funny!
- **Ethan Phillips**
Actor

Continued on next page...

Jim Pietsch's "NYC Cab Driver's BEST JOKE BOOK EVER!" is one of the funniest books I've ever read. But the story behind the book has a deeper meaning. It shows the true spirit of a New Yorker who just happened to drive a cab and asked all of his passengers to tell him jokes. The book shows the human side of New York, and celebrates how Jim got to know perfect strangers while making them (and now us) laugh hysterically!

> **- Christine Rucci**
> Fashion Consultant, *CEO of Godmother NYC Inc*

Jim strikes gold again, winning the marathon in the Joke Olympics. This book is funnier than a pole vaulter who lost his pants.

> **- Jeffrey Weinstein**
> Attorney at law

Jim Pietsch has earned the title of Jokester Extraordinaire, and has packed "The New York City Cab Driver's BEST JOKE BOOK EVER!" to the brim with the "Greatest Hits" of jokes. These jokes will not only leave you laughing, but will have you begging for more. And luckily, all you'll have to do is turn the page!

> **- BJ Leiderman**
> Theme Composer, *National Public Radio*

The New York City Cab Driver's BEST JOKE BOOK EVER!

WRITTEN AND ILLUSTRATED BY

JIM PIETSCH

PIETSCH
ART
BOOKS

ALSO BY JIM PIETSCH

The New York City Cab Driver's Joke Book

How to Remember and Tell Jokes

The New York City Cab Driver's Joke Book, Volume 2

The New York City Cab Driver's Book of Dirty Jokes

*This book is dedicated to all the
Joke Folk in my Joke World:
Past, Present, and Future.*

Preface

Jim Pietsch has a black belt in joke telling, and he has truly outdone himself with this newest compilation. His other books are hysterical, and I, like all of his fans, have been anxiously awaiting his latest.

"The New York City Cab Driver's BEST JOKE BOOK EVER!" is just that, and well worth the wait. No other book has made me fire Diet Coke out of my nostrils. I highly recommend that you read it, cover to cover, because all of the material will be on the final exam.

Laughter is best medicine, and thanks to Obamacare, Jim's books are available without a prescription.

~ Comedian Tom Cotter
The top *human* finalist on "America's Got Talent"

Acknowledgements

I drove a taxicab in New York City three days a week for over six years. During that time I met over 40,000 people and asked almost all of them for jokes. I must thank all the nice people I met on these city streets who told me their jokes, or listened to me tell them the latest one I'd heard. Literally thousands of people contributed to the creation of this book, and I want to thank them all for sharing their senses of humor with me.

Additionally, I had a number of joke parties with my best joke telling friends where I collected lots of great jokes. I must thank all of those participants who are too numerous to mention here, but you know who you are. I thank you from the bottom of my heart, not only for your jokes, but more importantly, for your friendship.

I also want to thank all the people who have come to my "Jam and Joke" parties where we play music and then take turns getting up to the microphone to tell jokes. To all my friends who played or listened to the music, and told or laughed at the jokes, I am grateful to you all for being an essential part of my world.

Additionally, I'm extremely thankful to all my friends and colleagues who continue to try to tell me a joke that I haven't already heard. Every once in a while, they get a joke through my "I know that one" filter and it lifts my spirits for days, weeks, or even months. And in this regard, I must give a special thank you to Hector Rios.

My Joke World was originally launched into the universe by Frank Baier, Christine Baier, and Patti Breitman. My three favorite joke tellers in the world are still (in order of their appearance in my life): Frank Baier, John "Ethan" Phillips, and Larry Bassen. Thank you all for bumping my life and laughter up to a whole new level.

I want to thank all the great people in my life who have, for many years now, given me the gift of their time, energy, guidance, and loyal friendship. I can't imagine life without you. Additionally, I have also met some wonderful people through my son Miles. Thank you to all of our PS3 and Clinton teachers and families, many of whom have become lifelong friends. And, of course, thank you to all my fantastic friends and colleagues in the HNC.

I would also like to thank Richie Cardenas for giving me my start as a professional musician. I've always been grateful to him for his patience as I was learning the ropes.

Thanks must go to Lorna Luft, who gave me some very insightful thoughts on women in comedy for my book, "How to Remember and Tell Jokes." She is one of the most intelligent people I have ever met, has a great sense of humor, and is blessed with a fantastic laugh to go with it.

A major thank you must go to Steve Kessler for all of his excellent business advice, as well as Howard Geltzer, the publicity guru. For their help with the final stages of the layout of this book, I must also thank Brae Singleton and Andy Bassford. Bob Waldman wrote the copy for the back cover, and I am very happy that his energy and spirit are part of this book.

Thanks to Bill Pietsch, Weezie Pietsch, Patti Pietsch, Shauna Wise, and Alea Wise, along with Ann Harris and all the Harrises, Kelleys, and Damones. You are the best family I could ever hope to have.

I am extremely grateful to my wife Mary Lou for her advice, encouragement, and support through the process of creating this book. Her contributions to our family cannot be overstated. I must also thank my son Miles, who has given my life an expanding amount of warmth, humor, love, purpose, and deep meaning…and now he's finally old enough to read one of my joke books!

Introduction

I had a fun-loving family when I was growing up, so one day after school when I was in sixth grade, I rushed home to tell my mother the new joke I'd heard on the playground. Here's the joke:

> A man and woman have just gotten married. They've decided to do it the old-fashioned way and not have sex before they get married, and now, tonight is their wedding night. However, they are not only very old-fashioned, but they're extremely bashful, so they're going to get undressed behind separate dressing screens.
>
> Just before they go behind the screens the man nervously says to the woman, "DON'T LOOK!"
>
> The woman says, "I won't. Don't YOU look!"
>
> The man says, "I won't."
>
> So they start to get undressed. The woman had bought a beautiful red negligee to wear on this very special night and had sent it to the cleaners. When she pulls it out of the box, though, she is very disappointed. The color of the negligee has faded, and it got all scrunched up in the box. She exclaims loudly, "OH, all PINK AND WRINKLY!"
>
> The man shouts out, "I TOLD YOU NOT TO LOOK!"

Knowing my mother, and the very open atmosphere we had in our family, I had thought that she would think this was funny. I was too young to have any inkling that she might be upset with an off-color joke. But when I hit the punchline my mother just burst out laughing. Then she said, "You'll have to tell that to Dad when he gets home."

When my father, a Presbyterian minister, arrived home that night, I ran right up to him and started telling the joke. He listened intently, and when I hit the punchline, Dad busted out laughing, too. I have always been grateful to my parents for reacting that day with acceptance and laughter, because at that very moment my lifetime of telling jokes began.

As the years went by, I enjoyed sharing jokes with my friends in junior high school and the musicians in my first rock band. After that, I traded jokes with the new friends I made in high school and college. During the summer between my first and second years at NYU, I hitchhiked around Europe. While taking an overnight boat trip from Rotterdam to England, my travel buddy and I met a couple of guys from Wales, and the four of us started telling jokes. We had a bunch of American jokes they had never heard, and they had a lot of Welsh jokes we had never heard. We wound up telling jokes the whole night long, laughing ourselves silly all the way to England. Here's a joke that one of the Welshmen told us:

Lord Nelson, the famous British naval commander, is standing on the bridge of his ship talking with his ensign. All of a sudden, the lookout from atop the mainsail yells down, "Four French frigates off the starboard bow!"

Admiral Nelson turns to his ensign and says, "Fetch me my red jacket."

His ensign replies, "But sir, if you wear red the enemy is sure to see you! It will be much easier for them to fire upon you from their ships!"

"Yes, yes," says the admiral, "but should I be hit, and should I bleed, the red of my jacket will absorb the blood and my men will think nothing is wrong and continue to fight."

The ensign says, "Of *course*! Very *good*, sir!" He snaps to attention, salutes smartly, and runs off to get the jacket.

He brings the red jacket back and Lord Nelson puts it on. About fifteen minutes pass, and the lookout atop the mainsail cries down, "*Forty* French frigates off the starboard bow!"

Admiral Nelson turns to his ensign and says, "Fetch me my brown trousers."

For some reason I can remember a joke for years, and can often remember the person who told it to me, and where we were when they told it.

When I became a professional musician (my instrument was the drum set: ba-da-boom!), my joke world escalated to a new level. Musicians, with their exquisite sense of timing, along with their enjoyment of performing in front of an audience, are outstanding joke tellers. Musicians trade jokes with each other at rehearsals, on breaks when gigging, during intermission when playing a show, or just meeting on the street. The jokes musicians tell are about any subject, but the ones that hit us the funniest are musician jokes, the more "inside" the better.

As a freelance musician in New York City, I had backed up Chuck Berry and Freddy King, played in many bands, played Off-Broadway and Off-Off-Broadway shows, and even performed a drum solo on a ten-foot platform on the Broadway stage in Bob Fosse's hit musical "Dancin.'"

And yet, like so many of us trying to earn a living playing music, there would be dry spells with no work, some longer than others. Maybe that's another reason why musicians tell jokes: the laughter is vital to survival.

One time I was booked on a recording session, and as we waited for them to get the studio set up, the guitarist told a joke.

A guy goes to the doctor and says, "Doc, I can't move my bowels."

The doctor says, "Okay, I have some pills here. Take two a day and come back and see me in a week."

The guy comes back a week later and says, "Doc, I still can't move my bowels."

The doctor says, "All right, here's some stronger medication. Take *four* of these pills, *twice* a day, and come back and see me in another week."

The next week, the guy comes in again looking very upset. "Doc, I *still* can't move my bowels."

The doctor says, "Wow, this sounds serious." He takes out his clipboard and says, "I had better get some more information about you. First of all, what's your occupation?"

The guy says, "I'm a musician."

The doctor looks very surprised. "A musician?" he says. "Why didn't you tell me that before?" The doctor reaches around toward his back pocket, takes out his wallet, and pulls out some bills. "Here," he says, "let me give you some money for some *food.*"

As is so often true with humor, sometimes you just have to laugh instead of cry.

During one of my extended lean times, I decided to drive a New York City taxicab so that I could become a little more financially solvent. For over a decade I had made my living exclusively through music, so when I had to drive a cab it felt like the worst thing that could be happening to me. But as it turned out, it was the best thing imaginable. Little did I know that driving a cab would spin my life off into a completely different direction. It was a direction that I could never have foreseen.

Before I got my hack license, I came up with a plan: I thought that it might help the grueling twelve-hour shift go a little faster if I asked all my passengers for jokes.

And so, from my very first fare on my very first day driving, I asked everyone who got into my cab, "Have you heard any good jokes lately?" The first thing that happened was that I got a huge surprise. Ninety percent of the people said, "I can't remember or tell jokes."

I was shocked. Joke telling had always come so naturally to me that I had always assumed everyone could do it, but I quickly found out that's not the case. Fortunately, on the other hand, the other *ten* percent of the people I asked were people like me, where if they knew one joke, they knew a hundred. Before too long, those kindred spirits started keeping me supplied with a multitude of hysterically funny jokes.

I heard jokes from grocery store clerks, international correspondents, prostitutes, flight attendants, lawyers, doctors, famous and struggling actors, musicians, writers, recording engineers, dancers, managers of famous recording acts, bartenders, waitresses, comedians, actors in soap operas, market researchers, cab drivers, tourists from all over the

United States and the rest of the world, florists, elderly women, beautiful women, drunken fraternity brothers, college students, gay people, straight people, travel agents, homemakers, Air Force pilots, surfers, book editors, priests, ministers, people in advertising, furriers, movie producers, television producers, Emmy Award-winning composers, party goers, outwardly seeming serious folks, club owners, restaurant owners, and English royalty.

And since New York is a major center of fashion, jewelry, textiles, publishing, film, television, music, theater, art, importing, exporting, banking, brokerage, finance and tourism, I had the unusual opportunity of meeting joke tellers from all over the country, even all over the world.

When I would ask, "Have you heard any good jokes lately?" and people said, "No," they would usually follow up with, "Have you?" At that point, I would be only too happy to tell them the latest joke I had heard. And I found that once you've shared a laugh with someone, you're sort of friends at that point. Then after telling a joke or two, I would ask people what they did for a living. I heard incredibly interesting (and sometimes intimate) stories about the fascinating lives of many thousands of amazing people here in New York City.

After discovering that my talent for telling jokes is somewhat rare, combined with the fact that I was hearing the best jokes in the world, I began to think that I should write a joke book and share the jokes with everyone. But I made a pact with myself. After a lifetime of looking through joke books in bookstores and only finding tame or lame jokes in them, I vowed that if I was going to write a joke book, it would *only* contain *actually funny* jokes.

I bought a small notebook and kept it with me in the cab. Whenever anyone would tell me a new joke, the next time I was stopped at a red light, or sitting in a traffic jam, I would jot down several words that would remind me of the joke. I remember the very first joke I put down in my note book:

Q: What would be one of the best things about
having a woman for president?
A: We wouldn't have to pay her as much.

*(Remember what I said before about laughing instead of
crying?)*

After six months of writing joke notes, I found that I was
only getting a new joke every day or so. Even though I was
collecting a lot of jokes, I calculated that at that rate it would
be a long time before I had enough jokes for a whole book.
So I called my best joke telling friends and announced I was
inviting them to a joke party. I explained that I was collecting
jokes for a book and told them that I would put a tape
recorder (remember those?) in the middle of the room and we
would all sit around in a circle and tell jokes.

On the appointed evening, as people arrived for the
party, they weren't even all the way in through the door
before the jokes started flying. I had to quickly leap across
the room and switch on the recorder. As we started getting
into telling the jokes, a spontaneous flow began to happen.
Someone would tell a joke about a giraffe that went into a
doctor's office. The next person would tell a joke about a
doctor who sees a lawyer, and that would lead to several
lawyer jokes, and on and on. It was like musicians playing
together, but instead of instruments we were jamming with
jokes. I was truly in my element, enjoying the hilarity of my
jokester tribe. After three hours of cackles, chuckles,
chortles, and guffaws, I had a whole slew of fantastic, brand-
new (to me) jokes.

The very next night I was back in the cab and a woman
hailed me at 102nd Street and West End Avenue. When I
asked her if she had heard any good jokes lately, she gave me
the best answer I had ever gotten. She said, "You go first."

After trading a few jokes with each other, she said, "You

know, *I'm* always the one telling jokes to people. It's so nice to have someone telling jokes to *me* for a change. You keep going."

It was a long ride, but I was armed with all the great jokes I had heard the night before. I kept her laughing all the way to 57th Street and Lexington Avenue. When we got to her destination, she said, "You know so many great jokes, you should write a book."

I said, "I'm going to," and showed her my book of joke notes.

She handed me her card and said, "I'm an editor for Warner Books. Give me a call."

I called her the next day and she told me how to write a proposal. Two weeks later, unannounced, I took the proposal up to the corporate headquarters of Warner Books. The receptionist called the editor and said, "Ms Breitman, I have Jim Pietsch, the cab driver, here in the lobby." Patti Breitman immediately came out to greet me. She said, "I'm so glad that you came!" She invited me into her office, and then sat down and read what I had written. She said, "This is *very* funny! And I really like the cartoons you did! Right now I'm heading into the meeting where we discuss what books we're going to publish next. I'm going to recommend this one."

The next morning, Patti called me with an offer. I was on my way to being a published joke book author!

Once the contract was signed, I began the process of selecting which jokes to include in the book. As I said before, I was only going to use *truly funny* jokes. However, as I was going through them, every now and then I would come across a joke that I thought was borderline funny and had to decide whether or not to put it in the book. Here is one of those jokes:

Q: Why do farts smell?
A: So deaf people can enjoy them, too.

I went back and forth on it for a while, then finally said to myself, "Ah, what the heck. I'll put it in." When the book

8

was eventually published, I gave a copy to a friend. After reading it, he said, "You know what my favorite joke in the whole book was? That one about why farts smell!" I was amazed. I always knew that humor is very subjective, but that really hammered it home. Then again, I have a friend who is fond of saying, "There's no such thing as a bad fart joke!"

After choosing which jokes to put in the book, I counted up my selections. Even though they were *all* good ones, I figured out that *one* out of every *three* jokes was an A#1 Primo Material Killer Joke. So when I put the jokes in order, I made sure that every third joke was one of the great ones.

When I finished the book, it went through all the preparatory phases, and then it was to be published at a printing factory in Buffalo, NY. I took the opportunity to visit a friend in Buffalo, and was able to watch my book coming off the presses! That was a huge thrill! As I was getting the tour of the printing factory, they told me that they had to put extra security on that day because my book was the kind of book that would get taken home by the workers.

When musicians play a song in front of an audience, they usually get applause when it's over. But when you write a book, you work like crazy putting it all together, and then when it's finally published...nothing! Your life just goes on as before. It was a little disconcerting. I once heard that a writer once described having a book come out as "the calm after the calm."

But I didn't have to wait too long before I started to get a few smatterings of "applause." A friend sent me a post card from Malaysia, saying that she saw my book in a small kiosk right next to the South China Sea! Another friend told me that she saw it in a store window in Stockholm, Sweden.

I got more applause when another friend told me that he had a dinner party and they all passed my book around at the table. He said that everyone took turns reading the jokes aloud, and they all had a rousing evening of raucous laughter.

Another friend told me that he was in a grocery store waiting in line for the cashier, and he saw that she was reading something to the cashier the next aisle over, making her crack up repeatedly. When he got to the front of the line, he saw that she was reading my book! Now, that's some applause!

Another friend was the cartoonist for the comic strip "Blondie." He told me that the wife of a friend of his had cancer, and so he would call her up every day and read her a joke from my book. Her husband told the cartoonist that his wife always looked forward to that phone call, and that it was the highlight of her day. Now *that's* what I call a standing ovation.

When I found out that my book had sold 50,000 copies, I immediately called my father. When he heard the news, he said, "Wait a minute. I have a ruler here, and I'm measuring how thick your book is. Your book is three-quarters of an inch thick." Dad took a moment to do a calculation, and then said, "If you piled up 50,000 copies of your book, it would be over *twice* the height of the Empire State Building!" Wow! The next time I looked up at the Empire State Building and visualized that stack of books, I was astounded. That's a *lot* of books! (And since then the total sales from all of my books have reached over *275,000* copies!)

One thing that I've always liked about having a published book is that sometimes I get the opportunity to give something back to people who have provided me with many years of entertainment. With that thought in mind, I waited outside the stage door when Jack Lemmon was on Broadway appearing in "Long Day's Journey Into Night." When Mr. Lemmon came out after the show I gave him a copy of my book. A week later I went back and asked him if he had read any of it. He smiled and said enthusiastically, "Yeah! There's some good stuff in there!"

I also gave a copy to the great magical comedy team of Penn and Teller, who were doing a show at the Westside Arts Theater. A couple of weeks after giving them the book, I went back and asked them if they had read any of the jokes. Penn Gillette said, "Yes! Every third joke is a really good one, so every night just before we walk out onto the stage, we have our stage manager read us three jokes from your book to put us in a good mood for the show."

On another occasion, I had both Robin Williams and Christopher Reeve together in my cab, along with their wives. It was the thrill of a lifetime, but that's another story for later in this book.

I should tell you, though, that namedropping is the *worst* thing you can do. Bobby DeNiro told me that.

After my first book came out we still continued having joke parties because they were so darned much fun. (I did record them, though, just in case…) At the end of one of the parties, after all my guests had left, I realized that we had just had a *great* party for several hours, where *everyone* was participating and laughing hysterically. And there was no alcohol or drugs! Once again, it hit me how joke telling is an extremely enjoyable and powerful activity.

Something else happened after my first book came out: I became a joke magnet. People were always trying to tell me a new joke, and I began hearing more and more really good ones. But because I didn't want to lower my standards of the humor quotient in my books, it took me twelve years before I felt that I had collected enough great jokes to write another edition. When I wrote The New York City Cab Driver's Joke Book, Volume 2, I once again counted up all the jokes. This time the ratio of the funniest jokes was one in every two! I guess my joke standards had gone up.

I did get the majority of the jokes in my first book from the passengers in the back seat of my cab. Many of the jokes in the second book were from driving a cab, too, but they were also from joke parties and from my ever-widening circle of joke telling friends. Now I've put all the A#1 Primo Material Killer Jokes from my two books together into one punchline packed volume: "The New York City Cab Driver's BEST JOKE BOOK EVER!"

As with all my previous books, along with the jokes, I have also included some of the funny true stories that actually happened in my cab. These stories are always in italics.

Some years ago I was playing drums in a show called, "Privates On Parade," which starred the Tony Award-winning British actor Jim Dale. Since then, Mr. Dale has gone on to be the Grammy Award-winning voice of the narrator and all the characters in the Harry Potter audio book series. Mr. Dale has always been a masterful joke teller, and he once told me that my first book was "his bible."

My hope is that this new book, "The New York City Cab Driver's BEST JOKE BOOK EVER!" will be the joke bible for the many thousands of my fellow jokesters out there in the world. When I was driving a taxi and asking my fares for jokes, a great many people said, "Man, I wish my brother was here, he knows a million jokes." Or "I wish this guy I work with was here. He comes in with a new joke every day! I don't know where he gets them all."

Even though nine out of ten people say they can't remember or tell jokes, a great many people *know* someone who is a joke teller. One of the great things about jokes is that *anyone* can tell them. Even people who can't remember or tell long story jokes can usually get off a good one-liner now and then. You don't have to be a professional comedian to generate hysterical laughter among your friends.

Comedians usually write their own material, and I had one tell me that professional comedians refer to regular story jokes and one-liners that we "normal" people tell as "street jokes." In my case, I think that's a fitting description since on the *street* is where I got so many of my jokes!

If you yourself are not a jokester, do yourself a favor and loan this book to a joke telling friend. It will come back to you tenfold. Because your friend, in the process of making the joke his own, will add personal improvements that will only make his telling of the joke even funnier.

If you, dear reader, *are* a jokester, please go out and spread these jokes around far and wide. Lord knows that we could use more laughter in the world these days. Furthermore, I am now on a quest to find the best joke tellers on the planet, so if you know a great joke that is not in this book, please post it on my Facebook page (**jimsjokezone**) where I will also post all the latest funniest things I find for all my friends to see. For jokes told on video, you can check out my YouTube channel: **Jim's Joke Zone**. If you want to easily order another copy of this book, or an eBook version, you can go to my website: **www.jimsjokezone.com** and click on the link to Amazon. On my website you can find more information about how to join me for Google Hangouts, where I can have real-time live video Joke Parties with my best joke telling friends all over the world. I hope that you will soon become one of them!

THERE'S NO SUCH THING AS AN *OLD* JOKE
IF IT'S ONE *YOU'VE* NEVER HEARD.

And now, without further ado,

Welcome to my Joke World!

A man is marooned on an island for ten years and has given up all hope of ever being saved, when suddenly one day a woman washes ashore. Her clothes are all tattered, and she is clutching a little waterproof bag. It seems that her ship also hit the coral reef off the island and has sunk. She, too, was the only survivor.

The man, overjoyed at seeing another person, blurts out his whole story, about how he managed to live on the island alone, learned to live off the land, and survived by his wits. When he has finished his story, the woman says to him, "You mean you've been on this island for ten years?"

"That's right," says the man.

"Tell me," she asks, "Did you smoke cigarettes before you were marooned?"

"Why, yes, I did," he says. "Why do you ask?"

The woman says to him, "Well, since you haven't had a cigarette in ten years, here!" And with that, she pulls a cigarette out of her little bag and gives it to him.

"Oh, wow!" he says. "Thanks a lot!"

As she lights it for him she says, "Say, were you a drinking man before you got shipwrecked?"

"Well," says the man, puffing on the cigarette, "I *would* have an occasional whiskey now and then."

The woman reaches into the little bag, and says, "You haven't had a drink in ten years? Here!" From her bag she produces a small flask and hands it to him.

He takes a pull from the flask and is thanking her when she suddenly says, "Gee, I just *realized*. You've been on this island for ten years. I guess you haven't, uh, *played around* in ten years either, have you?"

"Good God!" says the man. "Do you have a set of *golf clubs* in that bag?"

Last night I slept like a politician. First I'd lie on one side, then I'd lie on the other.

A surgeon, an architect, and an economist are having a discussion, and they begin to argue about whose profession is the oldest.

The surgeon condescendingly says to the other two men, "Well, you know that God took a rib out of Adam to make Eve, so I think that it's rather obvious that surgery is the oldest profession."

"Ah," says the architect, "but before that, out of total chaos, God made the heavens and the earth. So I think it's quite obvious that architecture is the oldest profession."

The economist merely folds his arms and smiles serenely. "And where," he asks, "do you think the total chaos came from?"

A man and woman are standing at a cocktail party when the woman says to the man, "You know, you look just like my *third* husband."

"Oh, really?" says the man. "How many times have you been married?"

The woman answers, "Twice."

Two pirates are sitting in a tavern, talking. One of them has a hook instead of a hand, and an eye patch. The other pirate has a wooden leg. After a couple of pints of beer, they decide to tell each other how they got their injuries.

"One day," says the first pirate, "we had pulled alongside a merchant marine ship and were boarding her. I had my sword drawn when suddenly a man with a saber caught me by surprise and chopped my hand off. So I had this hook put on. How did you lose your leg?"

"There was a terrific storm at sea," begins the second pirate. "I was on deck when a gust of wind blew the mast over. It fell on my leg, pinning me to the deck. The ship began to sink. I would have drowned if they hadn't cut off my leg and freed me. So I had this wooden leg put on. Now, tell me, how did you lose your eye?"

"Uh, well," says the first pirate, fidgeting, "I don't really want to talk about it."

"Come one," says the second pirate, "we made a deal. What happened?"

"Well," says the first pirate, "one day I looked up at he sky, and a seagull crapped right in my eye."

"A seagull crapped in your eye?" says the second pirate. "I can see how that would be uncomfortable and annoying, but it wouldn't cause you to *lose* the eye."

The first pirate replies, "It was my first day with the hook."

On one of my days off, I was taking a taxi myself, and talking to the cab driver. When I told him that I was also a

driver, he said to me, "I just love *this job, and I love it for* three *reasons: Number one, every day is payday. Each night when I get home I have that cash in my pocket.*

Number two, I'm my own boss. I can take a break anytime *and I've got nobody looking over my shoulder.*

Number three, I work when I want to. I used to get fired *for that!"*

Two employees are talking. One of them asks the other, "How long have you been working here?"

The other one replies, "Since they threatened to fire me."

A teacher standing in front of her class asks, "Children, what part of the human anatomy expands twelve times when it is directly stimulated."

Little Susie, in the front row, starts giggling and laughing, trying to cover her mouth with her hand. In the back row, Johnny raises his hand.

The teacher says, "Yes, Johnny?"

Johnny stands up and says, "Teacher, the iris of the human eye expands twelve times when it is directly stimulated by light."

The teacher says, "Very good, Johnny. That's the correct answer. And, Susie, you have a very dirty little mind; and when you grow up, you're going to be *very* disappointed."

A man walking down the street sees a restaurant with a sign over it. The sign reads:

WE PAY <u>YOU</u> $500 IF WE CAN'T
FILL YOUR ORDER.

So the man goes into the restaurant and sits down. He calls the waitress over and says, "Miss, I would like to order an elephant ear sandwich."

The waitress replies, "Just a moment, sir," and rushes back to the kitchen. She goes straight up to the manager and informs him, "Well, you had better get ready to pay that five hundred dollars."

"Why?" says the surprised manager. "What's wrong?"

The waitress tells him, "Some guy just walked in and ordered an elephant ear sandwich."

"OH, NO!" cries the manager, clutching his head. "Did we run out of elephant ears?"

"No," says the waitress, "but we ran out of those big buns we serve them on."

Q: What's the difference between L.A. and yogurt?
A: Yogurt has an active culture.

A teacher announces to her class, "Children, the student who can name the greatest man who ever lived will win this shiny red apple."

Immediately a boy from Illinois raises his hand.

"Yes, Bobby?"

"Abraham Lincoln!" says Bobby.

"Well," says the teacher, "Abraham Lincoln was a very great man, but he wasn't the greatest man who ever lived."

Right away a little English girl raises her hand.

"Yes, Martha?"

"Winston Churchill," says the little girl.

"Well, no," says the teacher. "Although Winston Churchill was indeed a very great man, he wasn't the greatest who ever lived."

From the back of the room little Bernie Goldstein raises his hand.

"Yes, Bernie?"

Bernie stands up and says, "Jesus Christ."

"That is *correct*, Bernie," says the teacher. "Come up and collect your apple."

When Bernie gets up to the front of the room, the teacher hands him the apple. "You know, Bernie," she says, "given the fact that you're Jewish, I'm surprised you said that *Jesus* was the greatest man who ever lived."

"Well, actually," says Bernie, "I *do* think *Moses* was the greater man, but business *is* business."

Q: What's the difference between a porcupine and a Cadillac?
A: A porcupine has the pricks on the outside.

Being a musician, writer, and artist, and all the while supplementing my income by driving a cab, I met many other struggling people in the arts. I finally got to the point where every time I met a woman who told me that she was an actress, I would ask, "Oh, really? Which restaurant?"

Most of them would reply with, "Unfortunately, you're right."

I could definitely relate.

A man says to his wife, "You never tell me when you have an orgasm."

The wife replies, "You're never home."

Q: What's the difference between Karate and Judo?
A: Karate is a martial art, and judo is what you use to make bagels.

Two friends who are struggling actors in New York City become taxi drivers to help support their artistic ambitions. After a couple of months of driving, one of the actors gets a part in a movie and is flown out to L.A. When the movie is released, it turns out to be a big hit and the actor goes on to become a big international movie star.

His friend, however, continues to drive a cab and keeps hoping for his big break. All the while, he closely follows his friend's career, sees all his films, and vicariously enjoys his success.

Ten years pass, and one day the famous actor is in New York on a promotional tour and he hails a cab. As luck would have it, the driver turns out to be his old friend, and they are both very surprised and happy to see each other.

After spending a few minutes catching up, the cab driver says to the star, "Lou, tell me something. We were in acting classes together for many years. We went to the same auditions, and at that time we were both fairly equal in our acting abilities. Yet you went out to Hollywood and became a great movie star, and I'm still here, struggling in New York, driving a taxi.

"Lou, is there anything that you have learned over the years that you could tell me about the acting profession? Something that would help me become more like you, a successful actor?"

"Yes, there is," replies Lou, "and I can sum it up in one word."

"Really?" the cabbie says with excitement. "Just one word? What is it?"

"Sincerity," replies Lou.

"Sincerity?" the cabbie asks. "That's it?"

"Yep," says the actor, "sincerity. Once you can fake *that*, you can do *anything!*"

Q: How can you tell when your home has been burglarized by gays?

A: When you come home, you discover that your jewelry is missing, and all your furniture has been tastefully rearranged.

B.B. King's wife decided that she was going to make his birthday especially memorable one year. The day before the party, she went out and got B.B.'s initials tattooed on her buttocks, one letter on each cheek. The next night, after his big birthday dinner with friends in his favorite restaurant, they went home. As soon as B.B. sat down in his favorite chair, his wife walked up to him and announced, "I have a big surprise for you." With that, she turned around, pulled up her dress, dropped her drawers, and bent over.

B.B. stared for a moment at the posterior just inches from his face, and then asked, "Who's BOB?"

An old woman wakes up one morning to find that the nearby river has overflowed and flooded her entire house. She cannot even go downstairs because the water has risen above the first floor. As she leans out her second-story window, she sees that the water is still rising.

Just then, a man in a rowboat happens to pass by. The man yells to her, "C'mon lady! Jump in! I'll save you!"

"No, thank you," says the woman, "the *Lord* will provide."

"All right, lady," says the man, "suit yourself," and he rows on.

The water rises, and the old woman must leave her second story and climb out onto the roof. She is sitting on her roof when a small motorboat with two men in it passes by.

"Come on, lady!" yells a man in the boat. "Jump in! We'll save you!"

"No, thank you," answers the woman. "The *Lord* will provide."

The boat motors on, and the waters rise. The woman climbs up onto her chimney, the only part of her house that is not completely submerged. A big motor launch comes by and stops near her. "Jump in, lady! Come on! We'll save you!"

"No, thank you," says the old woman. "The *Lord* will provide."

The boat drives away, and soon the water rises above the chimney and the woman drowns.

As she arrives in heaven, the rather annoyed woman demands to see God. When she is brought before him, she says, "Hey! What happened? I thought the *Lord* would *provide!*"

"For cryin' out loud, lady," says God, "I *sent three boats!*"

A man got into my cab one evening. He was middle-aged and distinguished-looking in a friendly sort of way. When I asked him if he had heard any good jokes, he told me this one:

A group of philosophy professors is traveling on a train in Scotland. They look out the window and see a black sheep grazing on the hillside. One of the men remarks, "Gee, I didn't know that the sheep in Scotland were black."

But another of the philosophers says, "Well, you can't really say *that*. You can only say that *one* sheep in Scotland is black. In fact, all you can say is that one *side* of one sheep in Scotland is black."

Yet another of the group adds, "Well, *really*, all you can say is that one side of one sheep in Scotland is black *some of the time*."

After hearing this joke, I said to myself, "This guy likes subtlety—a thinking man's jokester." So I returned with this joke:

Q: Do you know what the sadist said to the masochist?
A: Absolutely nothing.

He laughed and told me this one:

24

A medical student is taking a test and one of the questions is, "Name the three best advantages of mother's milk."

The student immediately writes, "One: It has all the healthful nutrients needed to sustain a baby. Two: It is inside the mother's body and therefore protected from germs and infections."

But the student can't think of the third answer. Finally he writes, "Three: It comes in such nice containers."

I then countered with this:

The optimist says, "This is the best of all possible worlds." The pessimist says, "You're right!"

The gentleman in the backseat beat me to the punchline on that one. He then told me this one:

This is a Russian fable: Once there was a man walking along a country road in the dead of winter. There was snow and ice all around, and the man, not having a warm enough coat, was shivering and hurrying to get home.

As he was walking, he happened to look down and see a little bird lying next to the road, all stiff and with its feet sticking straight up in the air. Feeling sorry for it, he bent over, picked it up, and put it inside his shirt next to his body, hoping that the warmth might help to bring it around. After about half an hour he felt a little flutter on his skin and was very happy that the bird was still living. But the man knew that what the bird really needed was warmth, something that he himself could not provide. Just then he happened to be walking by a cow pasture, and there, not too far from the road, was a steaming load that a cow had just dropped.

The man joyfully realized that this could provide the warmth that the bird so desperately needed. So he went over and stuck the little bird in the steaming pile. As he walked away he felt very happy with the thought that perhaps he had saved this little creature's life.

And sure enough, very soon the bird was revived by the warmth. He was so happy to still be alive that he let out a loud, clear song of joy. Now a fox happened to be stalking nearby, heard the song, and followed it to the bird -- and ate him.

Of course every Russian fable has a moral and this one has three: one) it's not always your enemies who get you into it; two) it's not always your friends who get you out; and three) if you're in it up to your neck, don't open your mouth.

An out-of-towner driving east on 46th Street at Madison Avenue pulls his car up next to a New Yorker and asks, "How far is it to Fifth Avenue?"

The New Yorker considers it for a moment, then tells the man, "The way you're going, about 24,000 miles."

A teacher says to her third-grade class, "Children, I'm going to ask each of you what your father does for a living. "Bobby," she says, "you'll be first."

Bobby stands up and says, "My father runs the bank."

"Thank you," says the teacher. "Sarah?"

Sarah stands up and tells the teacher, "My father is a chef."

"Thank you, Sarah," she says. "Joey?"

Joey stands up and announces, "My father plays piano in a whorehouse."

The teacher suddenly becomes very flustered and quickly changes the subject to arithmetic.

Later that day, after school, the teacher goes to Joey's house and knocks on the door. The father answers it and says, "Yes? Can I help you?"

"Your son Joey is in my third-grade class," says the

teacher. "What is this I hear about you playing piano in a whorehouse for a living?"

"Oh," says the father, "you see, actually I'm an attorney, but you can't tell *that* to an eight-year-old kid."

Q: What's the difference between a lawyer and a sperm cell?
A: A sperm cell actually has a one-in-two-hundred-million chance of someday becoming a human.

A priest, a minister, and a rabbi are talking to one another. They begin discussing the monies their respective organizations take in and how they divide these monies up.

The priest says, "Well, after the collection I draw a line on the floor. Then I throw the money up in the air. Whatever lands on the right side is God's and whatever lands on the left side is mine."

The minister says, "Yes, I use a similar method. I draw a circle on the floor, then throw the money up in the air. Whatever lands inside the circle is God's and whatever lands outside I keep."

They both turn to the rabbi. "How do you do it?" asks the priest.

"Well," says the rabbi. "I use a similar method. I throw the money up in the air, and whatever God wants he keeps."

A man dies and goes to Heaven. As Saint Peter is welcoming him at the pearly gates, the man confesses to the saint, "To be quite honest, sir," he says, "I'm really surprised to be here."

"Why is that?" asks Saint Peter.

"Well, to tell you the truth," says the man, "I never believed in this place. I never thought that Heaven really existed."

"That doesn't matter, my friend," replies the saint. "You see, up here we go by results. You were a good man, you were very generous, and you helped a lot of people. That's really all that matters. We don't care what you believed, as long as you led a decent, moral life."

Saint Peter continues, "However, I do have one problem. I'm just not quite sure where to put you."

"What do you mean?" asks the man.

"Do you see that big golden mosque over there?" Saint Peter asks, pointing to a cloud bank over to his right. "That's for the Moslems. That big marble temple in the cloud bank behind you is for the Jews, and that big wood-carved church over there is for the Presbyterians."

Saint Peter begins pointing all around. "The Hindus are

over there, Episcopalians over there, the Rastafarians actually *created* those clouds over there to the left—"

"Saint Peter," the man interrupts, "what's that big, tall, black building in that cloud bank over there behind you?"

"Oh," says Saint Peter, "that's for the Catholics."

"But why doesn't it have any doors or windows?" asks the man.

"Well," says Saint Peter, lowering his voice, "that's because they think they're the only ones up here."

Q: Did you hear about the new Japanese-Jewish restaurant?
A: It's called So-Sumi.

When I was younger, we used to tell jokes about a dumb guy, always called "The Moron." Then, when I got to junior high school, for some reason I never understood, the "Dumb Guy" jokes became Polish jokes.

Years later, when I traveled abroad, I learned that the English have Irish jokes (and vice versa), the Swedes have Norwegian jokes, Brazilians have Portuguese jokes, Texans have Aggie jokes, and so on. These jokes are usually based on some sort of rivalry, and it's a worldwide phenomenon. "Dumb Guy" jokes are popular because they are usually funny.

However, since I have never been able to find out any reason why we Americans tell Polish jokes, I've become very tired of slamming the Polish people. Therefore, from now on I am changing the "dumb guy" jokes to "Duddish" people from "Duddland." Here is one:

A Jewish guy and a Duddish guy are sitting at a bar, watching the news on the television. On the news they are showing a woman standing on a ledge, threatening to jump.

The Jewish man says to the Duddish man, "I'll tell you what. I'll make a bet with you. If she jumps, I get twenty dollars. If she doesn't jump, you get twenty dollars. Okay?"

"Fair enough," says the Duddish guy.

A few minutes later the woman jumps off the ledge and kills herself. The Duddish guy gets out his wallet and hands twenty dollars to the Jewish guy.

After about ten minutes the Jewish guy turns to the Duddish guy and says, "Pal, I just can't take this twenty dollars from you. I have a confession to make. This didn't really happen just now. I saw it on the news earlier this afternoon."

"No, no," says the Duddish man. "You keep the money. You won it fair and square. You see, I saw this on TV earlier today too."

"You did?" says the Jewish guy. "Well, then, why did you bet that the woman wouldn't jump?"

"Well," says the Duddish guy, "I didn't think she would be stupid enough to do it *twice!*"

Q: What do you get when you play a country song backwards?

A: You get your wife back, you get your job back, you stop drinking...

It is Barack Obama's second term in office and he receives a call on his red telephone in the Oval Office. When he picks up the receiver, he hears a voice on the line. It is President Putin of Russia. "Hello!" says the American president. "How are you?"

Putin says, "I'll get right to the point: I need to ask a favor of you."

Obama says, "I'll be happy to help if I can. What is it?"

Putin confides, "There has been a sudden rampant outbreak of AIDS in Russia, and it has gotten us pretty worried. We've run out of condoms. We need ten million more condoms right away, but our manufacturers just can't handle that kind of volume. Do you think that you could rush me a shipment of seven million condoms next week?"

Obama says, "I'll make some calls and see what I can do."

"Just one more favor," says Putin. "We need all the condoms to be sixteen inches long."

"I'll do my best and get back to you right away," says the President.

They hang up and Obama immediately telephones the largest condom manufacturer in the United States. When he gets the head of the company on the phone, he says, "Hello, this is President Obama."

The manufacturer is astonished. "Mr. President! What an honor to have you call! Is there anything that I can do for you?"

"Well actually, there is," says the President. "I need to ask you for a favor."

"Anything!" exclaims the manufacturer.

"I just got a call from Vladimir Putin, the President of Russia," Obama explains. "The AIDS situation has gotten out of control over there. It has them pretty scared and they need some more condoms. Could you ship out an order of seven million condoms to them as early as next week?"

"Of course, Mr. President," says the manufacturer. "It will require some rescheduling, and our factories will have to run twenty-four hours a day, but I think that we can handle it."

"Thank you, sir," replies the President. "However, I do have another favor to ask of you."

"No problem," says the manufacturer. "What is it?"

"Mr. Putin," says Obama, "has asked that you make all the condoms sixteen inches long. Could you do that?"

The manufacturer thinks for a moment, then replies,

"Well, it will involve retooling some of out machines, but for you, Mr. President, I am very happy to do anything that I can."

"There's just one more favor I'd like to ask of you." President Obama says. "On these seven million sixteen-inch condoms, I would like you to stamp in large letters, 'Made in U.S.A.—MEDIUM."

An eighty-year-old woman goes to the doctor and finds out, much to her great surprise, that she is pregnant. She immediately calls her husband on the telephone. "You old coot," she says, "you got me pregnant!"

The husband pauses for a moment, then asks, "Who *is* this?"

A teacher says to her class, "For our math problem today, I want you to figure out how many seconds there are in a year."

The children get out their paper and pencils and are just starting to get to work, when a Duddish kid in the back raises his hand. The teacher is quite surprised. "Dudley," she says, "do you know the answer already?"

"Yes, I do," replies Dudley. "There are twelve seconds in a year."

"Twelve?" asks the teacher.

"Yep," says Dudley. "January second, February second, March second..."

A newlywed couple is getting undressed on their wedding night. The husband, after removing his trousers, tosses them over to his new bride. "Put those on," he says.

The wife looks at him curiously. "What did you say?"

"Go ahead, put them on," he says.

"Well...okay," she replies, and she puts the trousers on. However, even after fastening the belt, they are still too large for her, and they just fall down around her ankles. "I can't wear these," she says.

The husband looks at her. "*All right*," he says, "now just *remember* that. I'm the one who wears the pants in this family. And don't you forget it!"

So the wife slips off her panties and throws them to her husband.

"Put those on," she says.

"What? What are you talking about?" he asks.

"Go ahead," says the bride. "You made me do it, now you go ahead and put *those* on."

"Well, okay," he says, and starts to put the panties on. But they're much too small, and he can't even get them up past his thighs.

"I can't get into these," he says.

The bride looks at him and says, "That's right— and you're not *going* to, either, until you change your attitude!"

Q: How many surrealists does it take to change a light bulb?
A: A fish.

One September evening in 1988, I was driving west on Twelfth Street when I saw a group of people coming out of a restaurant. As I slowed down to see if they would be needing a cab, I saw that one of the men standing there was Christopher Reeve. As I was watching him, he looked up, caught my eye, and hailed me. He then held up one finger, indicating for me to wait one minute.

As I sat in the cab, I saw that Christopher was with another man and two women. The man had his back to me as he put on his coat. He turned around, and as the group of people started walking toward my cab, I saw that the other man was Robin Williams.

Robin got into the back seat and sat between the two women, while Christopher opened the front door and sat down next to me. I couldn't believe my luck! They said that we would be making two stops. Once they had given me their first destination, I started driving and asked them if they had heard any good jokes lately.

Robin asked me the question of a one-liner, and I gave him the punchline. Everyone in the car laughed, and then I asked Robin a one-liner, and he replied with the punchline. We entertained the other people in the cab like this for several minutes (I'm proud to say that I held my own with Robin, neither one of us could stump the other) and then one of us told a recent Dan Quayle joke (which was the low-hanging fruit in the joke world back then).

This set Robin off on a routine about George Bush Senior (it was the day after Bush had gotten the date of Pearl Harbor wrong during a speech to a veteran's group). Robin started impersonating two veterans in the audience at Bush's speech: "September seventh, day of infamy? Oh yeah, that's was that weekend we took that shore leave."

I couldn't possibly try to recount his entire routine here, because it just wouldn't be funny without hearing Robin's rapid-fire delivery, including all the appropriate accents and sound effects. I will tell you, though, that it was as funny as anything I've ever heard him do on television or in a movie. The man was, without a doubt, a comedic improvisational genius.

A little bit later (fortunately, it was a fairly long fare), there was a momentary lull in Robin's hilarity, and I handed him a copy of my first book. "Check this out," I said. Robin opened it up and started reading jokes out of my book to the other passengers, making them all laugh loudly.

At one point, as Robin was reading the fifth or sixth joke, I looked over at Christopher Reeve laughing and thought to myself, "This is amazing! This has got to be one of my life's peak experiences! I have Robin Williams in the back seat reading material out of my book, cracking up Superman on the seat next to me!"

Robin then told me a very funny joke that was at the expense of a certain body-building comedian. After I stopped laughing at the joke, Robin said, "Don't tell anybody I said that. I can just see the headlines: "Man Who Works Out Kills Comedian In Hotel Room!"

After several failed attempts to tell Robin a joke that he hadn't yet heard, I got him with a musician joke that I heard from one of my teachers at the Berklee College of Music. Here's the joke:

A policeman is walking down the street when he sees a man holding a young boy by the shoulders and shaking him violently. The cop quickly walks up to them and says, "Hey! What's going on here?"

"Well, you see, officer," the man says, continuing to shake the boy, "I'm a bass player. I was playing in that club right there when this little jerk ran in and twisted one of the tuning pegs on my bass!"

"I can see why you're angry," says the policeman, "but is that any reason to *brutalize* the kid?"

The man begins to shake the kid even harder and says, "Yeah, but the snotty little brat won't tell me which one!"

He laughed enthusiastically, so I finally felt like I had upheld my honor.

When I got them to their first destination, I asked Robin to sign my book for me. He signed it, then he and his ladyfriend got out of the cab. Christopher Reeve went around and got in the back seat to sit with his woman friend, and as I was starting to pull away, I heard Robin shout loudly.

I stopped immediately, thinking that maybe he had forgotten something in the cab. I looked around, but he wasn't even looking in the direction of the taxi. I said to Christopher, "Was he yelling to us?"

Chtistopher turned around and looked at Robin, then turned back to me. "Nah," he said, "he was just working the room."

When we got to the final stop, I asked Mr. Reeve to sign my book, too. He did, paid me, and then he and his friend left. I opened up the book and saw Christopher Reeve's autograph. Then I looked up at the top of the page and saw that Robin had signed my book,

"You give great hack—Robin Williams."

A man is driving across the country, and somewhere in the Midwest he stops off in a small town to have a quick beer. He parks in front of a little bar and goes in. There are about eight or nine locals sitting around drinking, and as the traveler sits at the bar sipping his beer, he hears a man call out, "Twenty-seven!" Everyone in the bar bursts into laughter.

Another guy calls out, "Nineteen!" And again everyone laughs. The first guy calls out, "Thirty-six!" And once again everyone laughs. Everyone, of course, except the traveler, who is totally baffled. So he leans over to the bartender and in a low voice asks, "Hey, what's going on here? Why are these guys calling out numbers, and why is everyone laughing?"

"Oh," says the bartender, "you see, this is a very small town. Everyone here knows each other so well that they all know each other's jokes. So they just assign them numbers, yell out the number, and everyone knows which joke it is."

"Wow," says the stranger. "That's amazing! So after a couple more beers, he turns to the room and calls out, "Nineteen!"

There is a dead silence. He calls out, "Twenty-seven!" Nothing. "Thirty-six!" He's met with more silence. So he turns to the bartender and says, "Hey, I heard those numbers called out before, and everybody laughed. What's wrong?"

"Well, you know," says the bartender, "some people can tell 'em and some can't."

A guy walks out of a house of ill repute, and sits down on a park bench, deep in thought. "Man!" he says to himself, "what a business! You've got it. You sell it. And you've *still got it!*"

A huge, broad-shouldered mean-looking hulk of a man is in a supermarket. He goes to the fresh produce section and tells the produce clerk that he wants to buy just half a head of lettuce.

"You can't do that," the clerk tells him.

But the man says, "Oh yeah?" and tears a head of lettuce in half. When he goes to the front to pay, the cashier tells him that he'll have to check with the manager before he can sell the man just half a head of lettuce.

So the cashier walks over to the store manager, and says, "Some big, dumb-looking jerk wants to buy half a head of lettuce." Just then the cashier notices that the huge man has followed him to the manager's office, is standing behind him, and has just heard everything he said. Thinking quickly, the cashier points to the large man and tells the manager, "...and this kind gentleman has agreed to buy the *other* half."

After the man leaves, the store manager tells the cashier, "I like someone who can think on his feet. In fact, I want to train you to become a manager, so I am sending you up to Winnipeg, Canada for a training seminar."

"Winnipeg, Canada?" the cashier responds with a grimace. "The only people who come out of Winnipeg, Canada are either whores or hockey players!"

"I'll have you know," the manager says slowly, "that my *wife* is from Winnipeg!"

"Oh, really?" the cashier responds. "What position does she play?"

A guy goes to his doctor to get his test results. The doctor says, "We got the results back, and there's some good news and some bad news."

The guys says, "All right, give me the good news first."

"The good news," says the doctor, "Is that you only have twenty-four hours to live."

"That's the *good* news?" says the guy. "What could possibly be worse than that?"

The doctor says, "I've been trying to reach you since yesterday."

It was about four o'clock in the morning and I was nearing the end of my shift. My last fare had gotten out in Queens and I was driving back to Manhattan when I saw a traffic light that must have been broken, because it went straight from green to red. I slammed on the breaks and managed to stop before I entered the intersection, but as I screeched to a halt, I heard something thump behind me. It sounded like something had fallen off the back seat.

It sounded too heavy to be an umbrella, and besides, it wasn't even raining, so I stretched around and looked down. There, on of the floor of the cab, was an old brass lamp. I picked it up and as I looked at it, I noticed that it had gotten some dirt from the floor smudged on its side. So with the sleeve of my jacket, I tried rubbing the dirt off.

No sooner had I done that, smoke started pouring out of the lamp, and before I knew it, there was a genie sitting on the front seat right beside me. Before I could gather my wits about me, the genie said, "I am a genie and I am empowered to grant you one wish."

I just sat there stammering, until the impact of what he said struck me like a bolt of lightning. I knew immediately what I wanted. Without hesitation, I reached over into the glove compartment and got out a map of the world. I opened it up and said to the genie, "Do you see this? This is the world. My wish is that there will be peace all over the world for the next million years. No wars, no fighting, and everyone living together in kindness, generosity and brotherhood."

"Wow!" said the genie. "That's quite a tall order. Come on now. I'm just a genie. I mean, that's a really tough request! Isn't there something else you want? Some task that might be slightly less daunting?"

I thought for a few moments, and then said, "Okay, how about this? I wish to understand women. I want to know how they feel inside, what they're thinking, what makes them cry, and what makes them laugh. I want to know how to satisfy a woman in every way and make her happy forever!"

The genie thought for a moment, and then said, "Ummm...Let me take another look at that map."

Q: What's the difference between an oral thermometer and a rectal thermometer?
A: The taste.

An old Irish man is lying in bed, very ill. His son is sitting by the bedside, expecting the end to come at any moment. The old man looks up at the boy and says, "Son, I want you to go for the Protestant minister."

The son is totally taken aback. "But, Dad," he says, "you were raised a good Catholic! What in the world would ye be wanting with the minister at a time like this?"

The old man looks up and says, "Son, please. It's me last request. Get the minister for me!"

"But, Dad," cries the son, "you raised me a good Catholic. You've been a good Catholic all your life. It's the *priest* ye want now, not the minister!"

The old man manages to croak out the words, "Son, if you respect your father, you'll get the minister for me."

So the father prevails, and the son goes out and gets the minister. They come back to the house, and the minister goes right upstairs to the old man's room and converts him. As the minister is leaving the house, he passes Father O'Malley coming in the door at quite a clip.

The minister stares solemnly into the eyes of the priest. "I'm afraid you're too late, Father," he says. "He's a Protestant now."

Father O'Malley runs up the steps and bursts into the old man's room. "Pat! Pat! Why did ye do it?" he cries. "You were raised a good Catholic! We went to St. Mary's together! You were there when I performed my first mass! Why in the world would ye do such a thing at a time like this?"

"Well," the old man says as he looks up at his friend, "I figured if somebody had to go, it was better one of *them* than one of *us*."

A woman goes into a bar with a little Chihuahua dog on a leash. She sits down at the bar next to a drunk. The drunk rolls around, leans over and splat! He pukes all over the dog. The drunk looks down, sees the little dog struggling in the pool of vomit, and slurs, "I don't remember eating *that!*"

As I mentioned before, the Brazilians have Portuguese jokes. A Brazilian man once told me that the only thing in Brazil considered dumber than a Portuguese man is a Brazilian president. He then told me this joke:

A Portuguese man has an appointment to see the Brazilian president. He arrives two hours late, and the president is furious.

"Where were you?" says the president. "I've been waiting two hours!"

"I know, I'm sorry," says the man. "But I was riding up an escalator when it broke down. And do you know, I had to stand there for *two hours* while they fixed it!"

The Brazilian president throws up his hands in exasperation. "You idiot!" he yells. "Do you mean to tell me that you were *standing* on the escalator for *two hours* before they got it fixed?"

"Yes," says the Portuguese man.

"You stupid jerk!" says the president. "Why didn't you *sit down?*"

A very wealthy man says to his wife, "Honey, if I lost all my money, would you still love me?"

"Of course I would," replies the wife. "I'd *miss* you..."

Two lawyers are standing in bar. Suddenly, a beautiful woman walks into the room. One of the lawyers leans over to the other one and whispers, "Man, I sure would love to screw *her*."

The other lawyer whispers back, "Out of what?"

A drunk is driving through the city and his car is weaving violently all over the road. A cop pulls him over. "So," says the cop to the driver, "where have you been?"

"I've been to the pub," slurs the drunk.

"Well," says the cop, "it looks like you've had quite a few."

"I did all right," smiles the drunk.

"Did you know," says the cop, standing up straight and folding his arms, "that a few intersections back, your wife fell out of your car?"

"Oh, thank heavens," sighs the drunk. "For a minute there, I thought I'd gone deaf!"

I often get people in my cab who have just come from a movie or show, and many times I overhear their comments and reviews. On one occasion, however, a man and a woman were talking more about an audience member than about the dramatic Broadway show they had just seen.

43

"Wasn't that guy in front of us annoying," said the woman. "The way he was coughing and dropping coins on the floor every time he shifted in his seat? And always, of course, during the quiet moments of the show! You know, I counted seventeen coughs in the second act alone!"

"Yeah, I know," said the man, "and I counted a dollar eighty-five in change."

A Duddish man is sitting in a restaurant when all of a sudden a woman at the table next to him begins to choke on her food. It gets lodged in her throat so that she can't breathe at all, and she starts gasping for air. The people at her table all start to panic and don't know what to do, and the woman starts to turn blue.

Suddenly, the Duddish man leaps from his chair, runs over to the woman, pulls up her dress, yanks down her underwear, and starts running his tongue all over her bare butt. The woman is so shocked by this that she swallows really hard and her food goes right down.

The woman starts breathing again, and the people at her table all start to cheer. Then the friends crowd around the Duddish man. "You saved her!" they cry with joy. "You saved her life! How did you know so quickly what to do?" they ask.

"Aw," replies the Duddish guy, modestly, "that heinie-lick maneuver works every time."

Q: How does a musician make a million dollars?
A: He starts out with seven million.

Sometimes there's not much work around. In times like these, this is often especially true for ventriloquists. One day, two out-of-work ventriloquists are talking on the phone to each other (without moving their lips) and lamenting their condition. One of them, the older one who has been around the block a few times, says to the younger man, "Just between you and me, I've been moonlighting lately as a medium."

The young ventriloquist is quite impressed. "Really?" he says. "I didn't know that you were psychic!"

"Well, to tell you the truth, I'm not," confesses the older man. "But what I did was rent a storefront. Then I bought a small round table, a crystal ball, a turban, and put up a sign that said, "Psychic." When people come in, I throw my voice and they think that they're talking to their dead relatives."

"What a great idea!" says the young ventriloquist.

"You should try it too," suggests the first man. "You'll see, it works great."

The next day, the young man goes out and rents a little storefront, buys a table, a crystal ball and a turban. He opens up for business, and an hour later a middle-aged woman walks in. She sits down at the table across from the ventriloquist and asks him, "Can you put me in touch with my long-lost husband?"

"I sure can!" he answers. "Why, for just a hundred dollars, you can hear your husband speak to you from behind that curtain over there. Now, I must warn you that his voice might sound a little different, but that's because he's talking to you from the spirit world."

"That's wonderful," says the woman, eagerly.

"For a hundred and fifty dollars," the ventriloquist says, "you could have a two-way conversation with your husband, and talk back and forth with him."

The woman's voice rises in anticipation as she asks, "You mean, I could communicate directly with my dear departed Hubert?"

"Not only that," says the ventriloquist, getting just as excited as the woman. "For two hundred dollars, you could actually carry on a two-way conversation with your husband while I'm drinking a glass of water!"

Did you hear about the dyslexic rabbi? He was walking around everywhere saying, "Yo!"

A rabbit and a snake are traveling across a meadow when they bump right into each other. "Excuse me," says the rabbit, "I hope that you can pardon my clumsiness. It's just that I'm blind, and I didn't see you in front of me."

"That's all right," says the snake, "because I'm blind too. I can't see anything at all."

So they start talking and the rabbit says to the snake, "You know, because I've been blind since birth, I really don't even know what kind of animal I am. Could you maybe crawl all over me and tell me about myself?"

46

"Sure," the snake replies, "I'd be glad to."

The snake then crawls over the rabbit and when he's done the rabbit says, "Well, what am I?"

"You're furry," says the snake, "you've got a little cotton tail, and you've got long ears. You must be a rabbit."

"Wow, that's great," says the rabbit. "Thanks!"

"You're welcome," replies the snake. "As a matter of fact, I don't know what I kind of animal I am, either. Could you maybe do the same for me?"

"Sure," says the rabbit, and he begins to crawl all over the snake. When he's done he says to the snake, "Well, you're slimy, you've got a forked tongue, beady eyes, no ears, and no backbone. You must be a member of Congress."

Q: Did you hear about the Jewish kid who asked his father for fifty dollars?

A: His father said, "Forty dollars! What do you need thirty dollars for?"

A man and a woman got into my cab one night. I had to look twice at the guy to make sure he wasn't Woody Allen. It wasn't, but he looked just like him. I told him that last joke. When we arrived at his destination, I turned off the meter and said, "Okay, that will be ten-fifty."

The man said, "Six-fifty! That's a lot! Three-fifty is an awful lot for a cab fare!"

One day the pope gets a phone call from God. God says to him, "Since you have been such a good pope, I wanted you to be the first to know."

"The first to know what?" says the pope.

God says, "I have some good news and some bad news. The *good* news is that I have decided that from now on, the world will have only one religion."

"That's wonderful!" says the pope. "Now everyone will be peaceful and get along with one another. That's great! But what's the bad news?"

"In a few days," says God, "you will be receiving a phone call from Salt Lake City."

Q: If you're an American when you go into the bathroom, and an American when you come out, what are you when you're *in* the bathroom?
A: European.

Q: Did you hear about the new Duddish delicacy?
A: Pork tartare.

Dirty Ernie is sitting in the back of his first-grade class, a can of beer in one hand and a cigarette in the other. The teacher says, "Okay class, today we're going to play a game. I'm going to say a few words about something, and you try to tell me what I'm thinking about. Okay? Here we go.

"The first thing is a fruit, it's round, and it's red."

Little Billy raises his hand, and the teacher calls on him. Little Billy stands up and says, "An apple."

The teacher says, "No, it's a tomato. But I'm glad to see you're thinking.

"Now, the next one is yellow and it's a fruit."

Bobby raises his hand, and after the teacher calls on him, he stands and says, "It's a grapefruit."

The teacher says, "No, it's a lemon. But I'm glad to see you're thinking.

"Okay, the next one is round and it's a green vegetable."

Little Mary stands up and says, "It's a lettuce."

"No," says the teacher. "It's a pea. But I'm glad to see you're thinking." Then she says, "Okay, that's enough for today."

Just then, Ernie raises his hand and says, "Hey Teach, mind if I ask you one?"

She sighs and says, "Okay, Ernie. go ahead."

"All right," says Ernie, "I got somethin' in my pocket. It's long and it's hard and it's got a pink tip."

"Ernie!" shouts the teacher, "that's disgusting."

"It's a pencil," says Ernie. "But I'm glad to see you're thinking."

Q: How do you know that Jesus was Jewish?
A: He lived at home till he was thirty, he went into his father's business, he thought his mother was a virgin, and she thought he was God.

A man in my cab was a lawyer employed by Donald Trump. He told me that he was working on a project in which Mr. Trump wanted to develop a large area on the Upper West Side of Manhattan, right next to the Hudson River. There were plans to build a state-of-the-art television complex, and one of the buildings in the development would be the tallest building in the world.

The lawyer told me that the people in his office were talking about this building so often that they began to abbreviate the term "world's tallest building," by calling it the "WTB."

One night the lawyers were all in attendance at a town meeting to discuss this project, and since this was a very controversial issue, about four or five hundred people from the neighborhood had shown up. The lawyers kept referring to the building as the "WTB," forgetting that not everyone in attendance knew what the term meant.

Finally a woman stood up. She was a typical Upper West Sider, the lawyer told me. She had the whole outfit: the business suit and the running shoes. "Throughout this meeting," she said, "I've been hearing the 'WTB' this, and the

'WTB' that. Is this the 'QPS' that we're talking about here? Is that what it is, the 'QPS?'"

The lawyer told me that he turned to his associates and they were all asking each other, "'QPS'? Do you know what 'QPS' stands for?"

Finally, someone said to the woman, "What do you mean, 'QPS?'"

The woman replied, "Quintessential Phallic Symbol."

Q: What do George Washington, Thomas Jefferson, and Abraham Lincoln have in common?

A: They were the last three white men to have those last names.

A man is sitting at the bar in his local tavern, furiously imbibing shots of whiskey. One of his friends happens to come into the bar and sees him. "Lou," says the shocked friend, "what are you doing? I've known you for over fifteen years, and I've never seen you take a drink before. What's going on?"

Without even taking his eyes off his newly filled shot glass, the man replies, "My wife just ran off with my best friend." He then throws back another shot of whiskey in one gulp.

"But," says the other man, "*I'm* your best friend!"

The man turns to his friend, looks at him through bloodshot eyes, smiles, and then slurs, "Not any more!"

There is a young wrestler who beats everyone in high school, then college, so he decides to enter the Olympics. He does quite well, beating everyone, until there is only one match left and only one wrestler to beat: the Russian. Well, naturally, there is a big national hoopla about it. The Russian against the American for the world championship! There is much publicity and excitement about the contest, and everyone eagerly awaits the big match.

The day before it is to occur, the American's coach takes him aside. "Okay, look," says the coach, "you and this Russian are pretty evenly matched. But I have to warn you about one thing. This guy has beaten the last twenty people he's wrestled, and he's beaten them *all* with a move he's got called the Pretzel Hold. Once he gets you into this Pretzel Hold, forget it; there's no way out. So be careful. Keep mentally on top of it the whole match, and you can beat him. But remember: *watch out for the Pretzel Hold!*"

"Okay," says the wrestler. "Thanks. I'll be sure to keep on my toes."

The day of the big match comes, and the stands are full. All his friends and family are there, and all the lights, TV cameras, reporters, and eyes of the nation are on this contest.

The American and the Russian both get out on the mat and square off. They circle around each other a few times and then grab each other. They fall to the mat, locked in combat. It turns out to be a very exciting match. First it looks like the Russian will win, then the American. It keeps going back and forth like this for quite a while.

All of a sudden the American loses his concentration for just an instant, and WHAM! The Russian gets him into the Pretzel Hold. And he's got him; he has him pinned. The referee gets down on the mat and slaps the mat once! Twice! And *just* as he's about to slap the mat the third time, the Russian guy goes flying up in the air. He goes up so fast and comes down so hard that he is stunned for a moment. The American jumps on him, pins him, and wins the match.

The crowd goes crazy, everyone screaming and cheering. The stands erupt, and everyone swarms out onto the floor, surrounding the American. All the reporters are gathered around, and they say to the wrestler, "That was incredible! Fantastic! *No one* has ever gotten out of the Pretzel Hold before! How did you *do* it?"

"Well," says the wrestler, "I lost my concentration for just an instant, and that guy got me into the Pretzel Hold so fast, it made my head spin. I heard the referee slap the mat once, twice—and *just* as he was about to slap it the third time, I looked up and saw this testicle hanging there. So I *bit* it. And let me tell you, when you bite your own testicle, you'd be *surprised* what you can do!"

I told this joke to a man one evening, and he told me that it was his favorite joke back in the 1950s. He said that some of the details of the joke were different, but The Pretzel Hold was the same. It just goes to show that there's no such thing as an old joke, if it's one you've never heard.

A little boy gets up to go to the bathroom in the middle of the night. As he passes his parents' bedroom he looks through the keyhole. He watches for a moment, then continues down the hallway, saying to himself, "*Boy*, and she gets mad at *me* for sucking my *thumb!*"

A woman goes on a game show trying to win the top prize of $50,000. She keeps answering question after question and the prize money keeps building up. Finally she gets to the last question and the host says, "Okay now. For $50,000, here is your final question: What are the three most important parts of a man's body?"

Suddenly a loud buzzer sounds. "Oh, I'm sorry," says the host, "our time is up for today. We'll have to come back next week and ask you that question again. If you can answer it correctly, though, you will win $50,000!"

So the woman goes home that night and her husband is really excited. "Wow, honey!" he exclaims as he hugs her. "You did great! That was fantastic! And just wait until next week! We'll win $50,000!"

So the wife says to him, "Well, tell me, honey. What are the three most important parts of a man's body?"

The husband answers, "The head, the heart, and the penis."

"Oh, okay" she says. "Great!"

So for the next few days, the husband keeps testing her with the question. She's in the shower when he suddenly sticks his head in around the curtain and barks, "What are the three most important parts of a man's body?"

She quickly replies, "HEAD, HEART, AND PENIS!"

"Great!" says the husband.

All week long he keeps testing her, asking her in the strangest moments, and trying to catch her off guard. But she always gets the right answer.

Finally the big night arrives and she is very excited as

she arrives at the television studio. The lights go on, and as soon as they go on the air, the host says to her, "All right! You've had a whole week to prepare! Now...for $50,000...what are the three most important parts of a man's body?"

The studio audience falls to a hush. The hot bright lights are shining down, the cameras push in for a close-up, and the woman starts to get flustered. "Um...um...um...the..the...uh...the HEAD!"

"That's ONE!" says the host.

"Uh...uh...uh," stammers the woman, "uh... the HEART!"

The host shouts out, "That's TWO!"

Now the woman is so nervous that she can hardly think. "Oh, I know it, I know it," she says, "it's right on the tip of my tongue...I wish I could just spit it out...it's been drilled into me all week..."

The host says, "Aaah, that's close enough. You win."

I was driving behind a car and could see two women sitting in the front seat. The woman who was driving had a hair style that I can only describe as wild. On the back of the car there was a bumper sticker that read, "My only domestic quality is that I live in a house."

Q: What's the difference between a snowman and a snow-woman?
A: Snowballs.

A man goes into a bar, walks up to the bartender and says, "I'll bet you fifty dollars that I can bite my eye."

"All right," says the bartender, and throws his fifty dollars down on the bar.

The man proceeds to take out a glass eye and then bites it. As the man pockets the money he looks at the bartender, who has suddenly become very depressed.

"I'll tell you what," says the man. "I'll give you a chance to make your money back. I'll bet you double or nothing that I can bite my other eye."

The bartender thinks to himself. "Well, he can't have two glass eyes," and throws another fifty dollars on the bar.

The man then takes out his false teeth and uses them to bite his other eye. So the bartender begins to sink into a real gloom, until the man says to him, "Okay, I'll make you one more bet. I'll bet you this hundred dollars to five of your dollars that you can slide a shot glass down the length of this bar, and I can run alongside it and pee into it without spilling a single drop."

The bartender thinks, "Well, what have I got to lose," and says to the man, "Okay the bet is on," and he fully expects the man once again to have a trick up his sleeve.

So he slides the shot glass down the bar, and the man runs alongside, trying to pee into the glass. But rather than getting it in the glass, he misses completely and the urine splashes all over the bar.

The bartender is so happy to have won his money back that he throws his hands over his head and starts jumping up and down, laughing and cheering. Just then a man at a table over in the corner of the room slams his fist down on his table and begins cursing loudly.

"Gee," says the bartender, "I wonder what's the matter with *him*?"

"Oh, him?" says the man, handing the bartender the hundred dollars. "I bet *him a thousand dollars* I could piss all over the bar and make the bartender happy about it."

Two women are walking through the forest when they suddenly hear a voice say, "Ladies! Ladies!" They look all around them in the woods, but they don't see anyone. Then they hear it again. "Ladies! Ladies! Down here!" They look down and see a small pond with a frog sitting on a lily pad.

One of the ladies asks the frog, "Was that you?"

"Yes," is the frog's reply.

The two women are in shock. "How can you talk to us?" they ask. "You're a frog."

"I got turned into a frog by a wicked witch," explains the frog. "I'm really a fantastic jazz saxophone player."

"Really?" exclaims one of the women. "Is that true?"

"Yes," answers the frog, "and all it will take is one kiss from either of you, and I will immediately change back into a fantastic jazz saxophone player."

Right away, one of the women gets down on her knees, reaches out across the pond to the lily pad, and gently picks up the frog. Then she stands, quickly puts the frog in her pocket, and starts to walk away.

Her startled friend says, "Hey, wait a minute! Where are you going? He said that if you kiss him, he'll turn into a fantastic jazz saxophone player!"

"Are you crazy?" replies the other woman. "I can make a *lot* more money with a talking frog than I can with a fantastic jazz saxophone player!"

Q: How do you catch a unique rabbit?
A: Unique up on it.

Q: How do you catch a tame rabbit?
A: Tame way, unique up on it.

A black man dies and goes to heaven. When he reaches the pearly gates, he is met by Saint Peter.

"Welcome," says the saint. "You are about to enter the Kingdom of Heaven. Before I can let you in, however, I must ask you one question. What is the most magnificently stupendous thing that you ever did?"

"Oh, that's easy," replies the black man. "During the Mississippi-Alabama football game, underneath the grandstand, I boffed the granddaughter of the Grand Dragon of the KKK."

"Wow! That really *is* amazing!" exclaims Saint Peter. "Exactly when did you do that?"

"Oh," says the black man, "about five minutes ago."

An inveterate gambler is always spending money on gambling. Every dime that he gets, he blows it in Vegas or at the race track. One day his wife gets very ill, and she gets rushed to the hospital. The man goes to his friend. "You've gotta help me," he pleads, "I need some money to pay for these hospital bills."

His friend refuses. "I'm not going to give you money. You'll just blow it betting on the horses."

"No, I won't! I promise!" says the gambler. "I've *got* money for the horses..."

A family got into my cab one evening: a husband, his wife, and their teenaged daughter. As we exchanged jokes for a while I was, of course, limiting my selections only to clean ones.

When I got them to Tavern on the Green, the man, sitting nearest the door, got out first, then the daughter. As the wife slid across the backseat to get out, she paused a moment to lean over and say quietly into my ear, "Do you know why the Duddish man didn't enjoy his honeymoon?"

"No," I said.

"Because he was waiting for the swelling to go down," she said before getting out and rejoining her family.

Miss Smith, a society matron in Mobile, Alabama, has a problem. Several of her young female charges do not have dates for the big debutante ball coming up. Miss Smith tells the girls not to worry, that she will think of something to do about this.

She finally decides to call the nearby military base. When she is put through to the commanding officer, in her most charming southern accent, she says, "Sir, my name is Miss Smith and I am having a debutante ball this Friday night. Unfortunately, a few of my girls don't have dates for the dance, and I was wondering: would you be able to send a few of your officers over on Friday evening at eight o'clock?"

The commanding officer says to the woman, "Why, yes,

I think that some of our officers would love to attend your little soiree."

"Thank you so much," replies the woman. "And by the way, I do have two strict requirements."

"Yes?" asks the officer.

"Well, first," says Miss Smith, her accent making her sound like the Southern-belle that she is, "I want the men to be dressed in their finest dress whites, looking just as sharp as can be. My second condition is, of course, no Jews."

"It will be arranged," says the commander.

Friday night arrives, and the girls are all in the ballroom of the country mansion, dressed in their formal gowns. Several of the girls are without dates, standing alone. Precisely at the appointed hour, a jeep pulls up in front of the building. Six large black officers get out of the jeep, dressed in their finest formal white uniforms.

Miss Smith hurries over to them and says, "Can I help you men?"

One of the officers says, "Yes, Ma'am. We're here to meet our dates."

"Why...why..." stammers Miss Smith, "there must be some mistake!"

"No, Ma'am," says one of the officers. "You might make mistakes, and I might make mistakes, but Colonel Goldberg, he *never* makes mistakes."

America, through a twist of fate, suddenly finds itself with Donald J. Trump as the President of the United States. About a week after his inauguration, The Donald is lying in bed, staring at the ceiling. He thinks to himself, "This job isn't as simple as I thought. Could it be that I made a mistake for the first time in my life?" He's so freaked out that he can't sleep, so he decides to take a walk through the portrait gallery at the White House. He stops in front of Washington's portrait and says, "George, you were the father of our country. What can I do to best help the country?"

Suddenly, out of the portrait, a white mist appears. Trump is startled, and then completely amazed as the mist coalesces into the form of George Washington. Trump thinks to himself, "I never heard of this happening to anyone before. I guess it took Donald J. Trump to ask the question the *right way*." So once again he asks, "George Washington, what can I do to best help the country?" The form of Washington looks down at Trump and says, "Go to the people!"

Trump says, "Go to the people? Are you crazy? I tell the *people* what to do. They don't tell *me* what to do. Thanks, but *no thanks,* old man." The mist goes back into the painting, and Trump walks further down the hall.

He sees the portrait of Thomas Jefferson, and thinks to himself, "Hmm. Thomas Jefferson wrote the Constitution. *He'll* have a good answer for me." He goes up to Jefferson's portrait and says, "Thomas Jefferson, what can I do to best help the country?"

The mist comes out of the painting, and then the form of Thomas Jefferson's appears. He says, "Go to the Congress!"

Trump says, "Go to the *Congress*? Are you kidding me? They're all *losers*. Even the Republicans! They were going to try to deny me the nomination. Things were completely different in your day. *Your* Congress was the Founding Fathers. Those guys were *winners*. Things aren't like that any more. Thanks, Tom, but *no thanks*."

He walks a little further down the hall and comes upon The portrait of Abraham Lincoln. He says, "Aaah, Abraham Lincoln, you were the last great presidential statesman until *I* got elected. *You'll* have the right answer! Honest Abe, I know I can trust you. What can I do to best help the country?" The mist comes out of the painting, and the form of Abraham Lincoln takes shape. Lincoln gazes deep into Trump's eyes and says, "Go to the theater!"

A politician is walking down the street and he accidentally steps in dog poop. He looks down at his foot and cries out in distress, "I'm melting!"

While walking down the street one day, a national congressman is tragically hit by a truck and dies. His soul arrives in heaven and is met by St. Peter at the entrance.

"Welcome to Heaven," says St. Peter. "Before you settle in, it seems there is a problem. We seldom see a high official around these parts, you see, so we're not sure what to do with you."

"No problem, just let me in." says the politician.

"Well, I'd like to but I have orders from higher up. What we'll do is have you spend one day in Hell and one in Heaven. Then you can choose where you want to spend the rest of eternity."

"Really, I've made up my mind. I want to be in Heaven," says the congressman.

"I'm sorry but we have our rules." And with that, St. Peter escorts the politician to the elevator and he goes down, down, down to Hell. The doors open and he finds himself in the middle of a green golf course. In the distance is a club and standing in front of it are all his friends and other politicians who had worked with him. Everyone is very happy and dressed in evening dress. They run to greet him, hug him, and reminisce about the good times they had while getting rich at the expense of the people.

They play a friendly game of golf and then dine on lobster and caviar. Also present is the Devil (an honorary politician), who really is a very friendly guy who has a good time dancing and telling jokes.

They are all having such a good time that, before he realizes it, it is time to go. Everyone gives him a big hug and waves while the elevator rises. The elevator goes up, up, up and the door reopens in Heaven where St. Peter is waiting for him.

"Now it's time to visit Heaven." So twenty-four hours pass with the congressman joining a group of contented souls moving from cloud to cloud, playing the harp and singing. They have a good time and, before he realizes it, the twenty-four hours have gone by and St. Peter returns.

"Well then, you've spent a day in Hell and another in Heaven. Now you must choose where to spend eternity."

He reflects for a minute, then the congressman answers: "Well, I would never have thought it, I mean Heaven has been delightful, but I think I would be better off in Hell."

So Saint Peter escorts him to the elevator and he goes down, down, down to Hell. Now the doors of the elevator open and he is in the middle of a dark cave filled with piles of waste and garbage, and there are huge flames everywhere. He sees all his friends, dressed in rags, picking up trash and putting it in black bags. The Devil comes over to the politician and lays an arm around his neck.

"I don't understand," stammers the congressman. Yesterday I was here and there was a golf course and country club, and we ate lobster and caviar and danced and had a great time. Now it's just a rotten cave full of garbage and flames, and all my friends look completely miserable.

The Devil looks at him, smiles and says, "Yesterday we were campaigning. Today you've voted for us!"

Here is the musician's variation of that same joke:

A record producer dies and goes to heaven. He is greeted at the pearly gates by Saint Peter, who smiles and says to him, "I'm very happy to welcome you to Heaven." And with that, the gates swing open wide and the producer walks in. He is astounded to see that Heaven is a state-of-the-art recording studio.

The celestial studio is equipped with tube limiters, a fully digital mixing board with automated faders, wood carved walls, and speakers that are small, but clearer than anything the producer has ever heard on earth.

The producer has barely had time to regain his composure from the swoon that seeing all this unbelievably beautiful equipment has put him in, when Saint Peter says to him, "You are one of those rare individuals who has led such a good life on earth that we are now going to give you a choice. You may either stay here in Heaven and live out eternity with us, or you may choose to go to the other place."

"Wow!" exclaims the producer. "That's quite an offer! Not that I would be interested in going to the other place, of course, but...just out of curiosity, could I maybe take a peek and see what it looks like?"

"Certainly!" Saint Peter replies.

A trap door in the clouds near their feet opens up, and the producer looks down. He finds himself peering directly into the bowels of hell. What he sees is a long banquet table filled with food, including huge platters of steaks and pork chops. Crowded onto the long table alongside the bounteous food are many bottles of beer, wine, liquor, champagne, and of course, tequila. Around the table there are many people eating, drinking, and laughing hysterically. An incredible live horn band with many of the greatest musicians who ever lived is playing some funky, kick-ass R&B. Out on the dance floor are many beautiful, scantily clad men and women rocking to the irresistibly throbbing groove. At another table next to the stage is a large group of people smoking joints and doing lines of cocaine.

"Well," Saint Peter says to the producer, "what is your decision?"

"To tell you the truth, Pete," the producer says, "when I was alive, I worked pretty hard for many years. I kind of feel like I've already done the studio thing for a very long time. I'm really more into relaxing now, so I'm going to choose the other place."

"Suit yourself," is all that Saint Peter says before another trap door opens right below the producer's feet. The producer drops quickly down through a long, dark chute and before he knows it, he is thrown through a door and deposited onto the floor of hell. He looks around and all he sees are flames.

The devil is hiding behind the door, and as it slams shut, the devil takes a pitchfork and rams it up the producer's butt. He then lifts the pitchfork up and starts roasting the producer out over the flames.

The producer cries out, "Hey! Where's all the food and drink? Where's the band and beautiful women? Where's all the smoke and blow?"

The devil looks up at the producer, smiles, and then says, "Nice demo, huh?"

Q: How did Staten Island get its name?
A: In the 1600s, when the Dutch first saw it from their ship, they kept saying to each other, " 'S'dat an island?"

A young couple is living on a farm. One evening a flying saucer lands on the farm, right next to their house. Out of the flying saucer steps a young Martian couple, and they look very much like humans.

So the earth woman invites the Martians for dinner. They all sit down and start talking. They begin exchanging ideas and traditions, and they get to liking each other so much that they decide to switch partners for the night. The farmer and the Martian's wife go into one of the rooms, and the farmer's wife and the Martian man go into the other room.

As the Martian man takes off his pants the farmer's wife looks down and sees that his phallus is extremely small.

"What are you gonna do with that?" she says.

"I'll show you," he says, and proceeds to twist his right ear. Suddenly his penis extends to the length of one and a half feet. However, it is still only as thick as a pencil.

"That's pretty long," says the woman, "but it's really not very wide."

The Martian then reaches up, twists his left ear, and he becomes as thick as a huge sausage. They then proceed to have sex.

The next morning, the Martians take off and the farmer and his wife are having breakfast.

"So, how was it?" says the farmer.

"It was great," says the wife, "the best sex I've ever had! How was yours?"

"Well," says the farmer, "it was kinda weird. All night long she kept playing with my ears."

A heavyset man got into my cab carrying a guitar case. He was going to a theater, so I asked him if he was playing in the show's orchestra, and he said he was. So we started talking, and I told him which shows I had played. We then started exchanging musician jokes. He told me this one:

In the old West a wagon train is crossing the plains. As night falls the wagon train forms a circle, and a campfire is lit in the middle. After everyone has gone to sleep, two lone cavalry soldiers stand watch over the camp.

After a while, they hear war drums start beating from a nearby Indian village they had passed earlier in the day. The drums get louder and louder. Finally one soldier turns to the other and says, "I don't like the sound of those drums."

Suddenly, they hear a cry come from the Indian camp: "IT'S NOT OUR REGULAR DRUMMER."

I told the guitarist a couple more jokes, then he told me this one:

Two women are talking. One says to the other, "Say, you were going to go out with a French horn player. Did that ever happen?"

"Yeah," says the other woman, "it did."

"I remember you were really looking forward to it. How did it go?" asks the first woman.

"Well," says the other woman, "it went fine, and he's a really nice guy, but there's one major problem."

"Oh," says the first woman, "what's that?"

"You see," says the second woman, "every time he kissed me, he wanted to shove his hand up my butt."

We've all heard a lot of great Jewish jokes. Here are some Gentile jokes:

Q: Why did God create Gentiles?
A: *Someone* has to buy retail.

Q: Why do WASPs love to fly on commercial airlines?
A: For the food.

Q: What did the little WASP boy shout when he saw his school burning down?
A: "MY HOMEWORK!"

A very unusual situation arises at the most exclusive hotel in town. An Indian gentleman, the Maharaji of Sharma has checked into the grand suite. The entire staff is giving him the finest treatment with tremendous attention to every detail. At the end of the first week, he calls down to the front desk to order breakfast. "This is the Maharaji of Sharma, and I would like to order my breakfast for the morning."

The receptionist politely replies, "Yes, sir. You're a very special guest here at the hotel, and we hope you're enjoying your stay here with us. Whatever you would like to have, just say the word and it's yours."

"All right," says the Maharaji, "I'll get right to the order. What I would like to have for breakfast this morning is two pieces of toast. One piece of toast should be very dark. Black, breaking up as you put it on the plate. The other piece of toast should be almost raw. You know what I mean by raw toast? It should look like it did not touch the toaster."

The receptionist says to him, "I've never had an order quite like this."

"Yes," replies the Maharaji, "But this is exactly what I want. Next I would like to have two eggs. Bullseye eggs. You know what I mean, bullseye eggs? Good. But one of the eggs should be cold, cold as a witch's tit, and the other egg, the yolk should be splattered across the white in a very peculiar kind of pattern."

"Well," says the receptionist, "we're certainly going to do our best to please you with your order..."

The Maharaji continues, "Now I would like to get on to the bacon. I know that you serve bacon because you're not strictly kosher here. I would like to have two pieces of bacon. One piece should be to match the toast, black. The other piece of the bacon should be practically raw."

"Yes sir, that will be two pieces of bacon—"

"And to conclude this order," says the Maharaji, "I would like to have a cup of coffee."

The receptionist repeats, "A cup of coffee, yes sir—"

"Just a second," interrupts the Maharaji, "I want to give you the temperature of the coffee. I want it to be lukewarm."

"This is very unusual," says the receptionist. "We have hot coffee and we can serve you iced coffee on the side, if you wish. Any way that you would like it."

The Maharaji replies, "If I wanted hot or iced, I would have asked for it that way. No. I want it lukewarm."

The receptionist says to the Maharaji, "I think I have this order straight, sir. I'm not going to bore you by reading it back to you, but I must tell you, Maharaji, that as much as we wish to please you, this is a very unusual order. I'm not sure if we're going to be able to deliver this."

"I don't know why not," says the Maharaji. "I've gotten this order every day this week, and I didn't even order it!"

A man is calling on his best friend to pay a condolence call the day after the friend's wife has died. When he knocks on the door, he gets no answer, so he decides to go in and see if everything is all right. Upon entering the house, the man discovers his friend in the living room having sex with the maid.

"Jack!" says the man. "Your wife just died yesterday!"

His friend looks up and says, "In this grief, do you think I know what I'm doing?"

A woman once asked me if I knew what the three different types of orgasms are. When I said that I didn't, she explained them to me. "First," she said, "is the religious orgasm: 'Oh God! *Oh God! OH GOD!*' Then there is the positive orgasm: 'Oh yes! *Oh yes! OH YES!*' And the third type of orgasm is the fake orgasm: 'Oh Jim! *Oh Jim! OH JIM!*'"

Q: Did you hear about the Duddish lottery?
A: If you win, you get a dollar a year for a million years.

A busy executive goes to the doctor for a complete physical.

The doctor explains, "We have a new device that, with only a urine specimen, can tell us everything that is wrong with you."

"Great!" says the executive. "Let's do it."

The doctor gives the man a beaker. He goes into the men's room and comes out with a full container. The doctor then pours its contents into a small box with some dials and a small digital LED screen. The box begins to click and buzz and make strange sounds. After less than a minute the sounds stop and the doctor's iPad on the table starts to beep.

He picks up the tablet and studies it for a long time. Finally the man says, "What is it, Doc? Am I all right?"

"According to this," says the doctor, "You're fine except that you have tennis elbow."

"But that's impossible!" says the man. "I don't play tennis! I don't even play golf. I don't do anything like that!"

"Well," the doctor replies, "this digital device is never wrong. At least it's never been wrong yet. But I'll tell you what I'll do. You take this sterilized jar home with you tonight. Urinate into it tomorrow, first thing in the morning, bring it in, and I'll run it through the system once again, free of charge. How does that sound?"

"Fair enough," says the man.

As the executive is driving home he starts to think about the diagnosis and begins to get very angry about how the whole world has become so completely computerized and digitized. By the time he gets home, he has decided that he is going to "fix" that device.

He gets out of his car and pees a little into the jar. He then takes the dipstick out of his engine and swishes it around in the urine. Then he tells his wife and daughter what he's doing, and has them urinate into the jar, then catches some of his dog's pee in the beaker.

Finally, the next morning, before leaving home, he goes out behind a tree in his backyard and masturbates into the jar. He then drives into town, chuckling to himself.

"How are you this morning?" asks the doctor as he sees the man coming in.

"Fine, doc." He laughs.

"You seem to be in good spirits," says the doctor as he pours the specimen into the box. Once again it begins to click and buzz, and in less than a minute, the doctor's tablet begins to beep.

The doctor picks it up and studies it for a long time. The executive says, "So, Doc, heh, heh. What does it say today?"

"Well," answers the doctor, "according to this, your car needs an oil change, your daughter is pregnant, your wife has gonorrhea, your dog has worms, and your tennis elbow is going to get a whole lot worse if you don't stop jerking off like that."

A suspected foreign terrorist arrives at Kennedy Airport and is going through customs. He becomes extremely irate when the customs inspector insists on searching his bags. He screams at the inspector, "New York is the asshole of the world!"

"And I take it," replies the inspector, "that you're just passing through."

A couple is driving in the country. They have never had sex before because they have decided to do it the old-fashioned way and are waiting until after they are married. This night it happens to be raining really hard and the roads become dangerous, so they stop at a motel.

"We would like two rooms," the man says.

"I'm sorry, sir," answer the desk clerk, "but we have only one room available. But it does have two twin beds."

The couple look at each other and shrug. "Okay," says the man. "We'll take the room."

So they go in and he goes to his bed and she goes to hers. They turn out the lights and the woman says, "Honey, would you do me a favor, and please get me another blanket?"

The man says, "I have a better idea. Why don't we pretend we're married for fifteen minutes?"

She thinks for a moment, smiles, and then says to him, "Hmmmm...okay."

So he says, "Get up and get your own damn blanket!"

Q: What's the difference between a dead snake lying in the road and a dead lawyer lying in the road?
A: There are skid marks in front of the snake.

One night I overheard a discussion about shopping between two high school girls. One of them said to the other, "It must have been great growing up with a father who is the head of one of the largest department store chains in the area!"

"Well, it was kind of nice," answered the other girl, "because we got to go into the store and pick out whatever we wanted. The problem was that very often I didn't like the clothes that the store had, and we weren't allowed to wear anything that didn't come from my father's store.

"My mother used to cheat, though," the girl went on. "She used to buy clothes in other stores and then sew labels in them from dad's store. She never got caught, either!"

Q: What do you call the stork who brings Duddish babies?
A: A dope peddler.

A guy walks into a drugstore and goes up to the pharmacist. "Last Friday I ordered twelve dozen condoms, and when I got home, I found out I only got eleven dozen."

"Gee," says the pharmacist, "I hope I didn't spoil your weekend."

These two very old English gentlemen meet in their exclusive club in London. Over tea, the first man tells the other one, "Last year I went on a Safari to Africa."

"Oh, really?" says the second old gentleman. "Did you have a good time?"

"Yes," replies the first man, "it was wonderful. We went lion hunting. I remember at one point we were walking along the veldt area, I had my gun at my ready, and then we came upon this huge outcropping of rocks. I looked up, and up on top of the rocks I saw this huge lion ready to pounce. I went AAAGH! Well, I tell you, I just *pooped* in my trousers!"

The other gentleman says, "Well, yes, that's quite understandable. I probably would have done the exact same thing under the same circumstances."

"No, no, no," says the first man, "You don't understand. Not then! I did it just now when I went AAAGH!"

Q: What do you call a man and woman using the rhythm method of birth control?
A: Parents.

During the French Revolution a series of horrible murders was committed. The authorities were unable to determine exactly who the killer was, but they did manage to narrow it down to three suspects: A Frenchman, a German, and a Duddish man. Given the heinous nature of the crimes, they decided to execute all three men, just to make sure that the killer would never kill again.

On the execution day all the people gathered in the town square. The three suspects were brought together on the platform next to the guillotine. It was decided that the Frenchman would be the first to die.

"How do you want to lie in the guillotine?" asked the executioner, "face down or face up?"

The Frenchman stepped forward with dignity and said, "Since I am going to meet my maker, I would like to face the heavens as I die. I will go face up."

So they put the Frenchman in the guillotine face up and released the blade. The blade slid smoothly down, until just an inch above the Frenchman's neck, when it suddenly came to a complete stop.

"Free him! Free him!" cried everyone in the crowd. "The gods have spoken! He must be innocent!"

The executioner took the Frenchman out and let him go. Next he asked the German whether he wanted to go in the guillotine face down or face up.

"Since I have come from the earth and am going to return to the earth, I would like to face the ground as I die," said the German. "I will go face down."

So they put him facedown and released the blade. It slid down and once again, an inch above the man's neck, it suddenly stopped. The crowd cheered and called for the German to be released. "He is innocent!" they cried. "The gods have spoken!"

They took the German out and set him free. Finally they turned to the Duddish guy. The executioner looked at him and said, "Face down or face up?"

"What are you, crazy?" said the Duddish guy. "I'm not getting into that thing till they *fix* it!"

There is a variation on that previous joke where instead of a Duddish guy, the third guy is an engineer. When he gets in the guillotine face-up, he looks up, points, and says, "Hey, I think I see the problem."

Q: How do you get a tissue to dance?
A: You blow a little boogie into it.

Two ninety-year-old Jewish men, Moe and Sam, have been friends all their lives. Well, it seems that Sam is dying, so Moe comes to visit him.

"Sam," says Moe, "You know how we have both loved baseball all our lives. Sam, you've got to do me one favor. When you go, somehow you've got to tell me if there's baseball in Heaven."

Sam looks up at Moe from his deathbed and says, "Moe, you've been my friend many years. This favor I'll do for you." And with that Sam passes on.

It is midnight a couple nights later. Moe is sound asleep when a distant voice calls out to him.

"Moe..."

"Who is it?" He sits up suddenly. "Who is it?"

"Moe, it's Sam."

"Come on. You're not Sam. Sam died."

"I'm telling you," insists the voice. "It's Sam."

"Sam? Is that you? Where are you?"

"I'm in Heaven," says Sam, "and I've got to tell you some good news and some bad news."

"Tell me the good news first," Moe says.

"The good news," Sam tells him, "is that there is baseball in Heaven."

"Really?" says Moe. "That's wonderful. But what's the bad news?"

"The bad news," says the voice, "is that you're pitching Tuesday."

A husband and wife get ready for bed. After they get in bed the man gets up again, goes into the bathroom, and comes back with a glass of water and two aspirin. He gets into the bed and holds out the water and aspirin to his wife until she says, "What are those for?"

The husband says, "They're for you."

The wife says, "Why? I don't have a headache."

The man turns to her and says, "Gotcha!"

Q: What does a woman say after her third orgasm?
A: You mean you still don't know?

Q: What's the difference between erotic and kinky?
A: Erotic, you use a feather—kinky, you use the whole chicken.

Two men appearing to be in their early thirties got into my taxi. One of them was wearing a fedora hat and had a handlebar mustache that curled around at the ends. I told them a joke they really liked, and then I asked them what kind of work they did. The man with the hat told me that his job was working as a Japanese language translator.

When Japanese businessmen come to New York, this man gives them a tour of the city. Then he teaches them the local customs and how to get around. "Tell me," I said, "I've heard that the Japanese don't have much of a sense of humor. Is that true?"

"Well, they do," he replied, "but it's just very different from ours. I could translate a Japanese joke into English, but you just wouldn't get it. Even if you understood every word,

the humor just wouldn't translate. The same would be true the other way around. If you tried telling a Japanese person a joke in English, they wouldn't understand what was funny about it. Actually, that reminds me of a true story."

The man went on to tell me this story:

"I was living in Japan with my parents many years ago, and I met an American man in a night club. This was the most popular club in Tokyo, and the American worked as the M.C. for the shows. The club presented entertainers from all over the world, and one night the headliner was Sammy Davis, Jr.

"Before the show, Mr. Davis asked to speak with the M.C. in his dressing room. When the man got to the dressing room, Sammy explained to him that he was going to warm the audience up with a joke. He then told the American that he wanted him to translate it into Japanese.

"'Well, I don't recommend that you do that,' said the M.C. 'You see, they won't be able to understand the humor.'

"'No, no,' said Mr. Davis, 'this is a really good joke. They'll love it.'

"'But the humor just doesn't translate over here,' replied the M.C., trying to be as helpful as he could.

"But Sammy would have none of it. 'It'll go over great,' he said. 'You'll see.'

"As the M.C. went out onto the stage, he was sweating bullets. If Mr. Davis told the joke, he knew that it would fall flat and start the whole performance off on the wrong foot. If the show was a flop because of it, the man was very nervous about keeping his job at the club.

"He introduced Sammy Davis, Jr. to the Japanese audience (in Japanese, of course) to thunderous applause. Right away, Sammy began to tell the joke. He said a few lines, then paused and looked at the M.C., waiting for him to translate.

"In his best inner city dialect, the M.C. began speaking to the audience in Japanese. 'Ladies and gentlemen,' he said, 'Sammy Davis is now telling a joke and I'm supposed to be

translating it. I know, though, that the humor is so different that it won't translate, and it won't be funny to you.'

"He paused while Sammy told a few more lines of the joke. He then went on in Japanese. 'I'm really worried. If he doesn't get a laugh, I might be in trouble and lose my job.'

"Another pause while Sammy told a few more lines.

"I really need your help,' said the M.C. to the audience. 'When he comes to the punchline, I will count to three, and I want you all to start laughing.'

As the audience began to realize what was happening, some of the people began to chuckle. Hearing this, Sammy was encouraged, thinking he was going over great. With mounting enthusiasm, Sammy Davis got to the end of the joke and hit the punchline. The M.C. counted to three and the audience went wild with hysterical laughter.

"After the show, Sammy went up to the M.C., patted him on the back, and said, 'You see, Kid? I knew you could do it!'"

Q: How many feminists does it take to change a light bulb?
A: One, and there's nothing funny about it.

A Jewish funeral. Rubenstein has just died. There's a small collection of people there. The rabbi gets up and says, "Ladies and gentlemen. Ve're going to bury Mr. Rubenstein. I know he vasn't the most popular man in the neighborhood, but it's very important in the Jewish tradition that you have to say a few kind vords about a man before you can bury him. So I'm not going to talk about Rubenstein, I'm not going to be critical. Personally I didn't even know him. But if vun of you could be nice enough to say a few vords, ve'll get this over yipsy pipsy, and ve'll be done vit it."

There is a long silence. "Excuse me," says the rabbi, "Mr. Stein, I don't vant to bodder you, but you knew diss man, you lived near him for so many years, perhaps you could say a few kind vords."

Mr. Stein stares straight ahead. "I vouldn't say nothing."

"Excuse me," says the rabbi, "I don't vant to bodder you Mr. Kornblatt, but you vent to school vit Mr. Rubenstein, you vorked in the same business for so many years, you don't have to make a long speech, you don't have to make a eulogy, you don't have to be Shakespeare, but just a few vords, a sentence, two sentences, somzing, so ve can bury him and all go home."

Kornblatt says, "I've got notting to say about dat man, I don't want to talk about him. Vat I've got to say vouldn't help you, it's better I keep my mouth shut."

The rabbi says, "Ladies and gentlemen, I'm going to have to remind you, the Jewish people, it's a Jewish tradition, you can't bury a man, you can't put him in the earth forever unless somebody could say vun vord, a sentence, somzing, vun kind vord so ve can bury him. Ve'll be here forever. I vouldn't bury him, I'm telling you."

There is a long silence again. The rabbi says, "Look, Mr. Goldberg, maybe you could do a mitzvah for us all, you could just say vun kind vord. You knew him, you knew the family, just vun kind vord, Mr. Goldberg."

Goldberg looks up at the rabbi. "Everybody vants to go home," he says, "I'll say vun ting. His brother vas vorse dan him!"

Q: Did you hear about the bulimic bachelor party?
A: The cake comes out of the girl.

A nun is living in a very strict convent where they are only allowed to say two words every ten years. After her first ten years the nun very carefully considers what two words she will say.

She thinks about it and thinks about it, until they bring her before the Mother Superior. She then says to the Mother Superior, very slowly, "Bed's hard."

Ten more years go by, and once again the nun must decide what two words best describe her feelings. When she is taken in to see the Mother Superior, she once again speaks very slowly and says, "Food bad."

After ten more years, thirty years in all that she has been living in the convent, the nun once again thoughtfully chooses her two words. Slowly and deliberately she says to the Mother Superior, "I quit."

The Mother Superior says, "I'm not surprised! For thirty years all you've done is *bitch, bitch, bitch*."

Q: What's the best thing to throw to a drowning guitarist?
A: His amplifier.

A guitar player, a lead singer, and their road manager are in an elevator. They are riding down from the forty-third floor when the elevator starts making a loud screeching sound, and then suddenly comes grinding to a halt. They push buttons and alarms, but nothing seems to work. Finally, after standing in the elevator for twenty minutes, one of the guys says, "Man, I really wish we could get out of here!"

A large puff of smoke appears in the center of the elevator, and when it clears, the three guys are amazed to see a genie standing there. "Greetings," he says. "I am the Elevator Genie. I am empowered to grant three wishes, and since there are three of you, I will grant you each one wish." He turns to the guitar player and asks, "What is your wish?"

The guitar player thinks for a moment, and then says, "You know, at this very minute, the Rolling Stones are playing out at the Meadowlands Arena. I would give anything to be onstage jamming with them right now!"

"Oh, that's easy," replies the genie, and snaps his fingers. POOF! A cloud of smoke envelopes the guitarist. When the smoke clears, the guitar player is gone. The genie turns to the lead singer. "And what is your wish?" he asks.

The lead singer doesn't even have to think about it.

"Two weeks ago," he says eagerly, "we played a concert out in L.A. There was this blonde in the second row, and I just can't seem to get her out of my mind. I don't know her name, though, where she's from, or anything about her."

The genie smiles. "I know her name, where she's from, and right now she is lying on a California beach in a bikini. At the snap of my fingers, you will be immediately transported to that beach, lying right next to her." And with that, he snaps his fingers and POOF! The lead singer disappears. The genie turns to the road manager. "And what would you like?" he asks.

The road manager commands the genie, "GET THOSE GUYS BACK HERE, RIGHT NOW!"

Q: How many psychiatrists does it take to screw in a light bulb?

A: Just one, but the light bulb has to want to change.

Or the alternate version:

Q: How many psychiatrists does it take to screw in a light bulb?

A: What do *you* think?

A man goes to his golf club and, hearing that his regular caddy will not be in that day, hires another caddy. The day goes along pretty well, and the new caddy seems quite knowledgeable. Upon arriving at a fairway that has always been particularly tricky for the golfer, the man turns to the boy and asks, "Which club do you think I should use for this shot?"

The caddy says, "Sir, I know this golf course very well. The best club for this fairway is the five iron."

The golfer gets out his five iron, lines up his shot, and hits the ball. He smacks it really hard, and it veers way off to the right where his wife happens to be standing. It hits her in the head and she is killed instantly.

The wife is buried a few days later, and after the funeral, months and months go by before the man can even think about golf again. But after a year he thinks to himself, "I really loved the game. I shouldn't let it go out of my life. It was a freak accident. The game used to give me such joy. I should at least try to play once again and see how it feels."

He goes back out to the golf course, and as luck would have it, he gets the same caddy. Whey they get to that same fairway, he turns to the caddy and says, "Which club do you think I should use for this shot?"

The caddy says, "Sir, I know this golf course very well. The best club for this fairway is the five iron."

The man turns to the caddy and shouts, "You bastard! I played here a year ago and you told me to use the five iron and I *missed the green completely!*"

Two old Jewish men are sitting on a park bench. One of them says, "Today is the proudest day of my life. Today my son graduated from law school."

The other man says, "N.Y.U.?"

The first man says, "And why not?"

Two horses are talking and one of them says to the other, "You know, during the third race today, just as I was going around the curve at the far end of the track, I slipped on this muddy spot and fell down. I scraped my stomach and fell right on my balls. It really hurt!"

"You know, I don't believe it," says the other horse. "Today during the fifth race, I was going around that same curve and I slipped at that same spot, scraped my knees, and fell right on my butt. It was really painful! What a coincidence!"

A dog who happens to be walking by turns to the horses and says "I'm really sorry to interrupt, but I couldn't help overhearing what the two of you were saying. This is very strange. You see, I was in the dog race today, and just as I was going around the bend I slipped on a wet spot, scraped my nose and then fell right on my balls. It was excruciating! Once again, I'm so sorry to interrupt, but I just can't believe the coincidence!"

The dog walks off, and one of the horses turns to the other one and says, "What do you know about that? A TALKING DOG!"

A man down on his luck goes home to his wife and tells her, "Look, dear, we're low on money now, and we're going to have to cut down on some luxuries." He then adds scornfully, "If you would learn to cook, we could fire the chef."

"In that case," replies the woman, "if *you* would learn to make love, we could fire the chauffeur."

As unlikely as it may seem, a woman *actually told this to me. She said, "Did you know that PMS is mentioned in the Bible?"*

I was really surprised. "It is?" I asked incredulously.

"Yeah," she replied. "In the Bible it says, 'Mary rode Joseph's ass all the way to Bethlehem.'"

A barber is standing in his shop late one afternoon when a Duddish man walks in. The Duddish guy is wearing a pair of headphones and when he sits down in the barber's chair, the barber asks him, "Could you please take the headphones off now?"

The Duddish man gets a look of panic on his face. "Oh no!" he says. "I can't take the headphones off. If I do, I'll die!"

"Come on now," replies the barber, "you can't expect me to give you a haircut while you're wearing headphones."

"Just cut around them," the Duddish man says.

"That's ridiculous!" says the barber. "I'm not going to do that."

"All right," replies the Duddish man, as he starts to get up out of the chair. "I'll just go somewhere else."

"No, no, sit back down," says the barber, thinking of how slow his day has been. "I'll cut your hair." He proceeds to give the man a haircut, but it is very difficult cutting around the earphones, and takes him twice as long as a regular haircut. When he is done, the Duddish man pays him and leaves.

The next day, another Duddish guy comes into the

barber shop, and he is also wearing a set of headphones.

I was telling this joke to a friend, and when I got to this point in the joke, he interrupted me and said, "That poor second guy. He's in every joke, and he never gets to do anything. He's always just repeating the same thing that the first guy did, with maybe a slight variation, and then he's gone. He never gets to do anything original and never gets the laugh. I really feel sorry for that poor second guy."

So I would like to hereby suggest that we all pause for a moment and give a little mental "thank you" to all those second guys (and occasionally women) who do such an important, yet thankless job. We must remember that without them, we would not have that wonderful rhythm that is so essential to the payoff of our jokes. So I hereby (and I hope you join me) give my heartfelt gratitude to those tireless guardians of the all important "Three Rule" in joke telling. THANK YOU "SECOND GUYS" WHEREVER YOU ARE!

And now, back to the joke...

The barber says to him, "Are you going to take those headphones off so I can give you a normal haircut?"

"No, I can't!" exclaims the second Duddish guy with a look of terror. "If I take them off, I'll die! You have to cut around them."

The barber grumbles, but since it has been another slow day, he agrees to do it. Once again, it takes him a long time to cut the man's hair, and the barber is very frustrated with the difficulty of having to avoid the earphones.

The following day, another Duddish man walks into the barber shop and he is also wearing headphones. "Don't tell me," the barber says to him. "You can't take the headphones off or you'll die, so I have to cut around them. Right?"

The Duddish man looks relieved. "Yeah," he replies, "that's right!" He sits down in the chair and is expecting his haircut, but the barber is feeling extremely annoyed. The barber walks around behind the man, and thinks to himself,

"This is ridiculous. I'm gonna show this guy that he's not going to die if I take his headphones off." The barber reaches slowly up to the man's head, and then suddenly yanks the headphones off.

The Duddish man immediately clutches his throat with both hands, and starts making gasping and choking sounds. He starts to turn blue and then he falls out of the barber chair onto the floor. Within moments, the Duddish man is dead. The barber is totally shocked. "Oh my God!" he cries out. "What have I done?"

The barber suddenly realizes that he is still holding the headphones in his hands. He puts them up to his ears and he hears a voice saying, "Breathe in, breathe out...breathe in, breathe out..."

Q: How do you make holy water?
A: Put some water in a pan, and boil the hell out of it.

I had a friend who directed a TV show called, "Inside the Comedy Mind," which was hosted by Alan King. The director told me that Mr. King was talking to him one day about the different kinds of jokes. "There's the regular joke," said Mr. King, "with the setup and the punchline. Then there's the switcheroo, with the unexpected twist at the end. There's also the 'left turn joke...'"

At that point, my friend said, "Wait a minute. I'm familiar with the first two kinds of jokes, but what is a 'left turn' joke?"

Alan King thought for a moment, then said, "Okay, here's a 'left turn' joke," and told this one:

One afternoon, two friends happen to meet as they are walking down Broadway. One of them says, "Hey, Tom! How're ya doin'?"

Tom says, "Oh, hi Murray. Gee, I'm not really doing so well."

Murray replies, "What's the matter?"

"I just went to the dentist," explains Tom, "and he told me that I'm going to have to get my teeth capped. It's gonna cost me *five thousand dollars!*"

"*Five thousand dollars!*" exclaims Murray. "That's a lot of money! You should go see Dr. Feinman. As a matter of fact, his office is right up here on Broadway, just a couple of blocks north. He only charges five *hundred* dollars for a teeth capping job."

Tom says, "Five hundred compared to five thousand? Come on, we both know that you get what you pay for. How can it be so cheap? He must not be very good."

"No, he's great!" replies Murray. "He's—wait a minute! There's Al Cohen across the street! He had *his* teeth done by Dr. Feinman. HEY AL! COME HERE FOR A MINUTE!"

Al looks over from across the street, sees Murray, and comes right over. Murray introduces his two friends and then says, "Al, you had your teeth capped by Dr. Feinman, didn't you?"

"Yeah," answers Al, "I did. About a month ago."

Murrays says to Al, "Look, Tom needs to get his teeth capped, too. Tell him what kind of job Dr. Feinman did for you."

"Oh, okay" says Al. "Well, you know, all summer long my son and I have been trying to take a fishing trip together. Last Saturday we just decided on the spur of the moment to drive upstate to our favorite lake and rent a cabin and rowboat, to do some fishing before we completely miss the season. So we drove up there, but by the time we got to the lake, it was late in the afternoon. We decided, though, to go out for a couple of hours anyway.

"After sitting on the lake and fishing for a little while, we noticed some storm clouds brewing off in the distance. We didn't think much of it, but the wind was really strong that day, and before we knew it, the storm was right on top of us. We started to row back to shore, but it was really scary.

Lightning was cracking all around us, rain was pouring down, and huge waves were starting to kick up. Our little boat was being buffeted around on the waves, when one of the oars slipped out of the oar lock and went overboard.

"I knew that if we lost an oar in that storm, we'd be goners, so I reached out to try to grab it out of the water, but I lost my footing and slipped. My balls got caught in the oar lock and I was halfway out of the boat, hanging by my balls. It was unbelievably painful!"

Tom, who has been listening patiently to all of this, finally can't take it anymore. *"What the hell,"* he demands, *"does this have to do with your TEETH?"*

Al says, "Well, at that moment, it was the first time in months that I wasn't thinking about how much my teeth hurt."

Q: What is the mating call of a blonde?
A: "Boy, am I drunk!"

Q: What is the mating call of a brunette?
A: "Has that drunk blonde left yet?"

A ventriloquist is driving out to the West Coast for an engagement, but when he reaches New Mexico, his car begins to make a strange noise. He pulls into a service station in the middle of the desert and has the mechanic check it out. The mechanic says that he can fix it, but it will take about an hour. So rather than take a chance on being stranded somewhere, the man tells the mechanic to go ahead and repair the car.

The ventriloquist goes out in front of the gas station and is wondering how he is going to kill an hour in the middle of the desert. Just then, an Indian rides up on horseback. Next to the horse runs a dog, and behind are a dozen sheep.

"Ah," says the man to himself, "I can spend a little time having some fun with this Indian."

So he walks up to the Indian and says, "Sir, that's a mighty fine-looking horse. Do you mind if I ask him a few questions?"

The Indian eyes the man suspiciously and says, "*Horse no talk.*"

The man goes around to the front of the horse and says, "How do you like living with this Indian?"

Then, in his best horse voice he makes the horse appear to answer, "Gee, it's great! He feeds me well. He doesn't work me too hard. He takes real good care of me. I like him a lot."

Now the Indian is in total shock. He can't believe that his horse has just been talking. The ventriloquist then asks the Indian, "Do you mind if I ask your dog a few questions?"

The Indian looks sternly at the man and says, "*Dog* no talk."

But the man walks up to the dog and says, "So, how do you like having this Indian for a master?"

"Oh," says the ventriloquist in his best dog voice, "he's really nice. He always gives me enough food. He takes me hunting with him. His squaw is really nice too."

The Indian is now completely dumbfounded. He can't believe that the two animals he has had for years have suddenly begun talking.

Then the ventriloquist goes up to the Indian and says, "Look, I don't want to take any more of your time. But before you go, do you mind if I just ask your sheep one question?"

The Indian's eyes widen, and he says, "Sheep *lie*!"

Q: Did you hear about the Duddish actress?
A: She slept with the writer.

Three Frenchmen and an American woman are having dinner together. At one point during the conversation, the term 'savoir faire' is used by one of the Frenchmen. The American woman says. " Excuse me, gentlemen, but I don't know what that means. What is the definition of 'savoir faire'?"

"Ah," says one of the Frenchmen, "it does not translate directly into English, but I think I can give you a feeling for what 'savoir fare' means.

"As an example,' he continues, "suppose that a man

comes home unexpectedly from a long business trip. He goes upstairs to the bedroom, opens the door, and finds his wife in bed with another man. He says, 'Oh, excuse me.' That, my friend, is savoir faire."

The second Frenchman cuts in, "Pardon me, please, but that is not really the true meaning of savoir faire. It is very cool, I admit, but it is not savoir faire. Real savoir faire is when a man comes home from a long business trip, goes upstairs to the bedroom, opens the door, and finds his wife in bed with another man. The husband says, 'Oh, excuse me. *Please continue.*' Now t*hat* is savoir faire."

The third Frenchman says, "Ah, I must admit, that is very close to an accurate definition of savoir faire, but it is not quite right. Real, true savoir faire is when a man comes home unexpectedly from a long business trip, goes upstairs to the bedroom, opens the door, and finds his wife in bed with another man. The husband says, 'Oh, excuse me. Please continue.' If the man *continues...that* is savoir faire."

Q: Did you hear about the new Chinese restaurant that has really hot, spicy food?
A: It's called "Szechuan Fire."

After I asked a man one night if he had heard any good jokes lately, he said, "Yeah! Here is one I told to my boss the other night at a cocktail party."

A very dapper, well-dressed gentleman walks into a midtown branch of the JP Morgan Chase Bank one day and asks for a loan of $30,000 for two weeks.

The bank officer says to him, "Yes, sir, I think we can arrange something. I'll just need some identification and credit references."

"I'm sorry," says the very distinguished-looking man, "but I don't have either of those."

"Well, then," says the officer, "I'm afraid we can't help you."

"In that case," says the man, "I would like to speak to your boss."

He talks to the branch manager, who also tells him that a loan would be impossible. The man then demands to see someone higher up. This goes on and on, and the man is ushered in to see David Rockefeller.

"Yes, sir," says Mr. Rockefeller, "what can I do for you?"

"I need a loan of $30,000 for two weeks," says the man.

"And do you have identification and credit references?" asks Mr. Rockefeller.

"No, I'm afraid I don't," says the man. "However, I am willing to put up my Rolls-Royce as collateral." With that, he produces the keys to his car and drops them on the desk. "It is parked right out front."

"Well," says Mr. Rockefeller, "a $500,000 car as collateral for a two-week $30,000 loan is good enough for me." The two men shake hands, and the man is issued the check.

One week later he returns. He goes up to the officer he first spoke with and says, "I would now like to repay my loan."

The officer, upon seeing the man, snaps to attention. "Sir," he says, "I have strict instructions that when you come in, I should send you in immediately to see Mr. Rockefeller."

The man is once again ushered in to see David Rockefeller. He sits down and pays back the loan with $500 interest. Once they have concluded their business, Mr. Rockefeller says to him, "Sir, from the license plate on your car, I was able to run a check on you. You are one of the ten wealthiest men in the world! Why in the world would you want to leave your car here in exchange for a $30,000 loan?"

"Where else," says the man, "could I find such a great parking space so cheap?"

The man, upon finishing this joke, told me that when his boss heard it, his boss said to him, "Your timing is way off. You should have told me that joke two days ago. Yesterday I had lunch with David Rockefeller, and he would have loved it!" So, David, if it hasn't gotten back to you yet, I hope you're reading this now!

A Duddish carpenter is working on a building going up. He is on the second story using a chain saw when he accidentally slices off one of his ears. He looks down to the ground and, in hopes of finding his ear and having it sewn back on, calls down to the men working below.

"Hey," he shouts, "do any of you guys see an ear down there?"

One of the men glances around, then yells up, "Hey, buddy! Is this it?"

The Duddish guy peers down, then calls out, "No, mine had a pencil behind it."

Q: What do blondes and beer bottles have in common?
A: They're both empty from the neck up.

A man's father is very, very old, and the son can't afford very good treatment for him, so the old man is in a shabby, run-down nursing home. One day the son wins the lottery. The first thing he does is put his father in the best old age home money can buy.

His father is amazed at how beautifully run the place is. He can't get over it.

On the first day the old man is sitting watching TV, and he starts to lean a little bit to one side. Right away a nurse runs over and gently straightens up the old man. A little later the man is eating dinner, and when he finishes, he begins to tip a little bit to the other side. Another nurse runs over and gently pushes him upright again.

The son calls his father that night and says, "Well, Dad, how are they treating you there?"

"It's a wonderful place," says the father. "The food is gourmet, they have color TVs in every room, the service is unbelievable..."

The son says, "It sounds perfect!"

"It is," says the old man, "but there's just one problem. They won't let you fart."

Q: What do you call a guy who hangs around with musicians?
A: A drummer.

Your brother, your best friend, and you all die. You go to heaven, and as you enter the gates, an angel comes up and takes your brother by the hand. The angel leads him to a room, and there, standing in the room, is the ugliest woman he has ever seen. She is extremely fat, has greasy hair, and smells so bad, he can hardly stay in the room. The angel says to your brother, "As a reward for the way you spent your life, you must spend a hundred years with this woman."

The angel comes back out, takes your best friend by the hand and leads him to another room. There is the ugliest woman *he* has ever seen. She is just skin and bones with rotting teeth and warts all over her body. "As a reward for the way you spent your life," says the angel, "you must spend two hundred years with this woman."

The angel comes back out, takes you by the hand, and leads you to a room. Standing there is the most well-built, beautiful blonde you've ever seen. The angel turns to the blond and says, "As a reward for the way you spent your life..."

A man once said to me, "Remember, if it's got either tits or tires, it's going to cost you a lot of money and cause you a lot of heartache!"

A Duddish man is in New York on vacation and he gets into a cab. The cab driver notices that the man seems to have a sense of humor, so he decides to tell the visitor a joke. "Okay," says the cabbie, "I've got a riddle for you."

"Oh, great," says the Duddish guy, "I love riddles."

So the driver continues. "All right," he says, "here goes: I am my father's son but I'm not my brother. Who am I?"

The Duddish man scratches his head and thinks for a moment. Finally he says, "I don't know. Who are you?"

The cab driver says, "I'm me!

"Oh, right!" says the Duddish guy, "right! Say, that's pretty good!"

After his vacation, the Duddish man returns to his home in Duddland. One night shortly after he has gotten back, he is sitting around with some of his friends. "I heard a very good riddle when I was in America," he says. "See if you can figure this out: I am my father's son but I'm not my brother. Who am I?"

His friends look around at each other, but nobody can come up with the answer. Finally one of the friends says, "I don't know. Who are you?"

And the Duddish man says, "Well, strange as it may seem, I'm a cab driver in New York!"

Q: What do blondes and turtles have in common?
A: Once they're on their backs, they're screwed.

Q: Did you hear about the new restaurant on the moon?
A: Great food, but no atmosphere.

A man is walking down the street when a bum comes up to him and asks for a dollar. Being in a generous mood, the man pulls out a ten-dollar bill. As he hands it to the bum, he says, "You're not going to use this for booze, are you?"

"I never drink," replies the bum solemnly.

"I hope you're not going to use it for gambling," says the man.

"I never gamble," the bum replies in earnest.

"Say," says the man, "would you mind coming home with me? I would really like for my wife to meet you."

"Me?" says the surprised bum. "Why me?"

"Well," the man explains, "I would like to show my wife what happens to a man who never drinks or gambles."

101

A man asks his wife what she wants for her birthday. She replies, "I want a divorce."

The man replies, "Gee, I wasn't planning on spending that much."

A guy got into my cab one day, and after speaking with him for a few minutes, it turned out that we both play drums. After exchanging several musician jokes he told me this one:

Four guys are sitting at a bar, two at one end and two at the other. The first two men begin talking to each other, and their conversation starts with computers, then continues on to politics and world affairs. When the discussion turns to the stock market, one of the two men says to the other, "You know, I really like you. What's your IQ?"

The second man says to the first, "It's 135. What's yours?"

"It's 140. No wonder we get along so well. Say, there's a lecture on nuclear physics being held a few blocks away from here. What do you say we leave this place and go?"

"Great!" says the other man. "Let's do it!"

As they walk out, there are two other men at the far end of the bar sitting with their beers in front of them and their heads hanging.

The first one says to the other, "Did you hear that?"

"Yeah," says the second man.

"What's your IQ?" says the first one.

"Twenty-five," says the second.

"Mine's thirty," says the first one. "What size sticks do you use?"

A true drummer's joke...or so I thought. Since then, however, I have heard this joke told many times in many variations, from guitarists ("What size strings do you use?") to actors ("Been to any auditions lately?")

Two psychiatrists who are friends happen to run into each other on the street one day. One of them says to the other, "You're fine. How am I doing?"

A man is sitting in a cafe in Mexico, trying to decide what he wants to order, when a waiter walks by. On the plate he is carrying are two big round hunks of meat, about the size of grapefruits.

The man calls the waiter over, points to the plate, and says to him, "*That's* what I want!"

"I'm sorry, sir, but that is the special, and there is only one order of the special available each day."

"What kind of special is that?" asks the man.

"You see, sir," says the waiter, "those are the balls of the bull killed today in the bullfight. It is our most popular item, and one must reserve it many days in advance."

"When is the next free day?" asks the man.

The waiter checks his book and says, "Tuesday."

"All right, then," says the man, "put me down for Tuesday."

So each day the man eats at the cafe and sees the huge bull balls being delivered to the eagerly waiting customer.

Finally Tuesday arrives, and the man excitedly goes to the cafe and sits at his regular table. "I'd like the special, please," he says, and sits back, anticipating a wonderful meal.

When the waiter arrives, though, on the plate there are just two small pieces of meat hardly larger than grapes.

"Hey, what is this?" says the man.

"I'm sorry, sir," says the waiter, "but you see, the bull doesn't *always* lose."

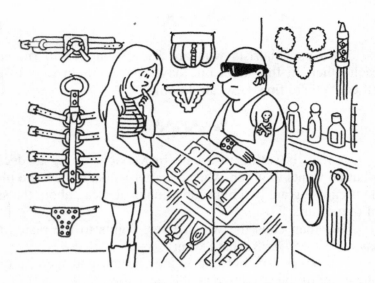

A woman goes into a sex shop and after looking around for a while, she asks the man behind the counter, "How much are the dildoes?" The clerk reaches into the display case and pulls out a box. He takes the dildo out of the box and stands it up on the glass counter top. "This white dildo here is fifteen dollars," he says.

The woman looks at it for a moment, and then asks, "What else do you have?"

The man reaches into the case again and pulls out another box. "This black dildo here" he says, "is twenty five dollars." He takes the black dildo out of the box and stands it on the counter.

The woman picks up each dildo, feels it for a moment, and then asks, "How much is that plaid dildo over there on that shelf behind you?"

The clerk turns around and looks at the shelf behind him. "Oh, that's an expensive one," he says. "That one costs seventy-five dollars."

"Hmmm," the woman says, thinking it over. "You know what? I'm going to take the plaid one." She pays the man the seventy-five dollars, and leaves.

A few minutes later, the owner of the store comes in and notices the two dildos standing on the counter. He says, "Have you been selling some dildos today?"

"Yes, I have," replies the clerk.

"How many have you managed to move?" asks the owner.

The clerk answers, "Well, I sold five white dildoes at fifteen dollars apiece, I sold seven black dildoes at twenty-five dollars apiece, and I managed to get seventy-five dollars for your thermos!"

Q: You are in a room with a mass murderer, a terrorist, and a lawyer. All you have is a gun with two bullets in it. What do you do?

A: Shoot the lawyer twice.

Frequently, people will ask me if I have heard the latest weather forecast, and I always have to tell them the same thing: "I never pay attention to what the weathermen say. I find that they are wrong so often that you would be just as well off if you flipped a coin."

It is still amazing to me that with all their sophisticated equipment they are unable to predict the weather any more accurately than they do. One night I was talking to a woman, and we were in total agreement about this whole issue.

I said to her, "I don't know of any other job where you can be wrong so often and get paid so much."

"You're right," she agreed. "As a matter of fact, the only difference between us and the weathermen is that we have windows!"

Q: What's the difference between mashed potatoes and pea soup?

A: Anyone can mash potatoes.

Louie is talking to his friend and says, "Guess what? *Everyone* in the world knows me."

"*Sure* they do," says the skeptical friend.

"But," Louie insists, "it's true!"

"Oh, yeah?" the friend answers. "Well, I bet Tom Hanks doesn't know you."

"Okay, come on," says Louie. He takes his friend to the airport. They fly to California and go out to the studio where Tom Hanks is just finishing a take on the movie he is now shooting. Tom looks up and, seeing the two men approaching, runs up, shouting, "Louie! Louie! How have you been?" He gives Louie a big hug and insists on taking the two men to lunch.

After Louie and his friend have had lunch, they leave the restaurant and the friend says, "Okay, Tom Hanks knows you. But that doesn't mean *everybody* does. I'll bet your own senator doesn't know you."

"Come with me," says Louie.

The two men fly to Washington and go into the Capitol. As they enter the Senate chamber, Louie's senator stands up and says, "Gentlemen, Louis is here."

The senators all jump up and cheer, crowding around Louie. They adjourn for the day and take Louie and his friend to dinner. The friend is very impressed.

After dinner the friend says to Louie, "All right, I admit that probably everyone in this country knows you. But what about Europe? I bet Steffi Graf doesn't know you."

The next day the two men fly to Germany. At the airport they happen to run into Steffi Graf, who is on her way to London. "Louie!" says Steffi, "I'm sorry, but I'm just leaving Germany. Say, why don't you and your friend come to

London for a week as my personal guests?"

At the end of the next week, as Louie and his friend are sitting by the pool, the friend says, "Well, Louie, a lot of people certainly seem to know you. But you say *everybody* knows you, and I bet the pope doesn't know you."

The next day they fly to Rome. When they get to the Vatican, Louie walks up to the gate, and he is let in for a special audience with the pope. Louie tells his friend to wait in St. Peter's Square.

As the friend is standing in the square the pope comes out onto the balcony. The crowd lets out a roar. Then Louie follows the pope out onto the balcony and the crowd lets out another roar. As Louie and the pope are standing arm in arm waving to the crowd, Louie looks down and sees his friend faint.

Louie runs down into the crowd and gets to his friend just as the friend is coming to.

"What happened?" says Louie. "Was it too much for you that the pope knew me too?"

"That *was* very impressive," says the friend, rubbing his forehead. "But what really got to me was when a man came up to me, tapped me on the shoulder, and said, "Hey, who's that guy with Louie?"

◆▪◆▪◆▪◆▪◆

A Chinese man and a Jewish man are drinking at a bar. After a little while the Jewish man leans over and gives the Asian man a strong punch in the arm.

The Chinese man is very startled and exclaims, "What's *that* for?"

"That was for Pearl Harbor," says the Jewish man.

"Pearl Harbor was the *Japanese*. I'm *Chinese*!" the Oriental man replies.

"Ah," says the Jewish man with a wave of his hand, "Japanese, Chinese, what's the difference?"

A little while later the Chinese man leans over and gives the Jewish man a hard punch on the arm.

"Hey," says the Jewish guy, "What was *that* for?"

"That was for the *Titanic*," the Chinese man says.

"The *Titanic*?" asks the bewildered Jew. "That was an *iceberg*!"

"Ah," says the Chinese man, with a wave of his hand, "Iceberg, Goldberg, what's the difference?"

Three women die at the same moment and are standing in front of Saint Peter at the gates of heaven. Saint Peter says to the first woman, "How much money did you earn during your last year on earth?"

The woman answers, "I worked at an investment banking firm on Wall Street and I earned two million dollars."

Saint Peter turns to the second woman and asks her the same question. "Well," she replies, "I was an executive at a large cosmetics corporation and I made five hundred thousand dollars."

"And how much did you earn?" Saint Peter asks the last woman.

She replies, "I made eight thousand dollars."

"Oh," says Saint Peter. "Ballet, jazz, or tap?"

A little boy runs up to his mother and shouts, "Mommy! Mommy! I want to be a drummer when I grow up!"

The mother sweetly replies, "You can't do *both*."

An Englishman got into my cab one night and told me to take him to a certain address on West 72nd Street. "That's just a few doors down from the Dakota," I said, "where your fellow Englishman, John Lennon, used to live."

"Yes, I know." replied the man. "My ex-wife was standing ten feet away from him when he was shot. My main regret is that the blighter had such bloody good aim."

"This was your ex-wife?" I asked.

"Yes," he said. "I'm in the middle of a lawsuit with her. She is still using my title, quite illegally, you understand. But with your ridiculous American divorce laws she got an estate that had been in my family for three centuries, and so I had to buy it back from her. Even that I could tolerate, but I won't allow her to continue to use my title."

"What is your title?" I asked.

"I'm an English lord," he said. "You know, Americans are so impressed with titles. I don't mind, really, but I did get rather annoyed at a party once when this American woman kept calling me Mister Lord."

"A lord, eh?" I said. "Well, I must say, I'm impressed. I guess that means that I'm an American."

"Yes," said his Lordship, "you probably are. You know, one day a friend of mine in the houses of Parliament was walking up a staircase on the side of a great hall. My friend, a well respected lord in Parliament, looked across the hall and saw the Lord of Limerick going down the staircase on the other side.

"The Lord of Limerick had just come from a photo session, and was wearing his ermines and all his jewels. My friend needed to talk to the Lord of Limerick about a debate that was soon going to be occurring in the Houses of Parliament. Since these two lords are of the same stature, my friend could address the other lord by his first name.

"So he called across the hall to him, 'Neil!' The Lord of Limerick did not hear him, so my friend called out again, this time louder, 'NEIL!' At that moment, fifty American tourists got down on their knees. The next day, that story made the front page of the London Times!"

Q: What do you get when you lock a gay guy and a Jewish guy in a closet?
A: They come out with a musical.

A man goes to the doctor, and the doctor tells him that he only has twelve hours to live. When he goes home and tells his wife, she cries and cries for a long time. Then she holds him and announces, "I'm going to make this the best night of your life."

He says, "It's the last."

And she says, "But it'll be the best!" So she lights candles, makes his favorite dinner, and opens a bottle of their favorite champagne.

They have a wonderful dinner and then go straight to bed. They make love, and just as they're about to fall asleep, he taps her on the shoulder and says, "Honey, could we do it again?"

So they make love again, and just as she's about to fall asleep, he taps her on the shoulder, saying, "Sweetheart, could we do that once again?"

So they do it again, and just as she's about to fall asleep, he taps her on the shoulder and says, "Darling, could we please just do that one more time?"

The woman replies, "Sure! What do you care? You don't have to get up in the morning."

Q: Why did the Duddish guy return his necktie?
A: It was too tight.

A Duddish guy decides that he wants to try ice fishing. He gets a fishing rod, a stool, a bucket of bait, and a saw. He goes out onto the ice, puts the bucket down, sits on the stool, gets out his saw, and is about to start cutting, when a deep, loud voice comes booming out from overhead: "DO NOT CUT A HOLE IN THE ICE!"

The Duddish guy is startled and quickly looks straight up. Then he looks all around him, but he doesn't see where the voice is coming from. He then replaces the saw on the ice and is about to begin his first cut, when the loud voice once again booms out, "DO NOT CUT A HOLE IN THE ICE!"

The Duddish guy jumps up, looks all around, then up in the air again, but he still can't figure out where the voice is coming from. So he settles back in, and is about to start cutting for the third time, when the voice commands, even louder this time, "I REPEAT! DO NOT CUT A HOLE IN THE ICE!"

Now the Duddish guy is certain that the voice is coming from directly overhead. He looks up and says, "Who are you?"

The voice answers loudly, "THIS IS THE RINK MANAGER! DO NOT CUT A HOLE IN THE ICE!"

Q: What's the difference between a wife and a mistress?
A: About twenty-five pounds.

Q: What's the difference between a husband and a boyfriend?
A: About forty-five minutes.

A woman goes into a toy store and picks a Barbi doll up off the shelf. As she's looking at it, the store manager happens to walk by. "Excuse me, sir," the woman asks the manager, "does Barbi come with Ken?"

"No," the manager replies, "Barbi *fakes* it with Ken. She *comes* with G.I. Joe!"

In the late 1940s, a couple from New York travels to Budapest for their honeymoon. On their last night there, they are walking around the streets and quaint back alleys of the Old World city, when they come upon a small theater. On the marquee it reads:

Appearing Tonight! The Great Shlomo!

The young couple goes in and they find themselves in a tiny little theater with folding chairs and about three people in the audience. There is a small spotlight illuminating the stage and as the newlyweds take their seats, a pretty female assistant in a skimpy costume comes out and places three walnuts on a table. She then walks unceremoniously offstage. The couple hears an announcer's voice coming over a small, tinny loudspeaker, "Ladies and gentlemen, The Great Shlomo!"

The small red curtains part, and out comes a short, little man who resembles Dracula, with the slicked-back jet black hair and a big long cape. The Great Shlomo, with a flamboyant fanfare, whips open his cape, and reveals a huge penis with a massive hard-on the size of a large sausage. He walks up to the table, and with his hard-on he quickly cracks open the three walnuts BOOM! BOOM! BOOM! Then the music hits a resounding TA-DAAAAH! There is a smattering of applause and the show is over.

Fifty years later, the couple decides that they want to relive their honeymoon and so they go back to Budapest. It is their first time in the city in fifty years, and at the end of their week there, they are walking through the streets, discussing how much the city has changed. They see a narrow street that looks familiar, so they turn down the little lane. What should they see but the same small theater from so many years ago. The marquee reads:

The Great Shlomo!

They turn to each other. "Could it be?"

"Maybe it's his son!"

"We have to go see."

They walk into the tiny old theater, and it looks the same, except that it looks fifty years older. Some of the folding chairs are broken, the spotlight is rather dim, and they are the only two people in the audience. As they sit down, they see the rather dumpy looking female assistant in her skimpy let-out costume slowly hobble over to the center of the stage. She takes out three coconuts, places them on the table, and walks slowly offstage. As soon as she is in the wings, a raspy voice comes through the crackling speaker, "Ladies and gentlemen, The Great Shlomo!"

The tattered, faded, red curtains part, and out comes The Great Shlomo. His hair is now white, and he also is moving very slowly. Once he gets to the table, though, he suddenly whips open his cape and there is the same massive hard-on. BOOM! BOOM! BOOM! He cracks open the three coconuts in rapid succession.

The couple can't believe it. They decide that they must talk to this man. When the house lights come up they make their way backstage in order to meet The Great Shlomo in his dressing room. The wife says to him, "Shlomo! We saw you fifty years ago on our honeymoon. We can't believe that you're still at it!" Shlomo smiles and nods appreciatively.

"There's one thing that puzzles us, though," the husband says. "Fifty years ago you were cracking open walnuts. Now you're cracking open coconuts. How come?"

"Well," says The Great Shlomo in a soft voice, "Many years have passed, and to be quite honest, my eyesight isn't what it used to be."

A man once said to me, "My penis is four inches. Now *some* women like it, but some women *don't* like it that wide."

The international scientific community comes up with an innovative experimental project. They decide to put all of the greatest minds in research together for three full weeks They set them up in a research facility with everything they need, including state-of-the-art laboratories, and the most advanced high-tech equipment available.

This project is an attempt to see what can happen if these scientists are allowed to work together in a positive environment, and to freely share ideas in the spirit of international cooperation.

After the second week, one of the scientists leaps up from his lab table, holding a test tube high in the air. "Eureka!" he cries. "Eureka! I've found it! THE CURE FOR CANCER!"

Suddenly, the scientist clutches at his chest and falls over. As he hits the floor, the test tube smashes and the fluid spills out all over the floor. The other scientists rush over to their colleague and find him dead of a heart attack. They quickly try to mop up the liquid from the test tube with a cloth, but it is too late. The fluid has evaporated.

They rush over to the scientist's notes, but it is page after page of indecipherable scribbles and no one can understand them. The scientists all begin to wail and moan. "Oh no! This is terrible! We had it!! We had the cure for cancer! And now it's lost! Oh no!"

The director of the program is in the next room and hears all the commotion. He rushes in and says, "What happened? What's the matter?"

Some of the scientists are openly weeping, others are pounding the tables, and some are lying on the floor groaning.

"What is it? What is it?" asks the director.

One of the scientists looks up from the floor and sobs, "We had it! We had the cure for cancer, and then we lost it. This is terrible! This is just awful!"

"Hey, hey, hey! Calm down now," says the director. "Just relax. I mean, we're not making *movies* here."

A maitre d' goes over to a middle aged Jewish couple eating in his restaurant. He asks them, "Is anything all right?"

A man is walking down the street when he sees a person with four arms and antennae coming out of his head. He goes up to him and says, "You're not from around here, are you?"

"No," says the person with the antennae.

"You know," says the man, "I don't think you're an American, either. As a matter of fact, I don't think you even come from this *planet!*"

"Right again," says the person with the four arms. "I'm from Mars."

"Well," says the man, "that's quite some configuration you've got there, with those four arms and those antennae and everything."

"Thank you," the Martian answers. "We Martians all have them."

"Well, that's just amazing," the man replies. "And, say, what is that big, round, gold plate there in your chest? I've never seen that before. Do all Martians have those?"

"Well, no," says the Martian, "Not the *goyim.*"

One night I stopped at a diner to have dinner. In the men's room, this was scrawled on the wall:

Dyslexics of the world—Untie!

A farmer has a rooster that goes around screwing all the animals in the barnyard. The rooster keeps this up for quite a while before the farmer finally pulls him aside and warns him. "Look," the farmer says, "you had better take it a little easier or you're liable to screw yourself to *death*."

The rooster just laughs at the farmer and goes out and has all the chickens in the chicken coop. He then goes through all the cows, then the pigs, and so on, until he has been with all the animals on the farm.

He keeps this up every day for weeks. Then one day the farmer doesn't see the rooster around the barnyard, so he goes looking for him. Out above one of his fields, the farmer sees some vultures circling around and around. The farmer runs out and sees the rooster lying spread-eagled on the ground.

"I knew it!" says the farmer. "I knew this would happen to you! Oh, why didn't you listen to me when I warned you?"

The rooster opens one eye, points upward, and says, "Shh. they're getting lower."

Two Duddish guys are walking down the street. One of them suddenly stops short and says sadly, "Wow! Look at that dead bird." The other Duddish guy looks up in the sky and says, "Where?"

118

An actor calls up his agent and says, "Hello, is Sid there?"

The secretary says, "Oh, I'm sorry, uh, but you see, Sid passed away last Friday."

"Oh," says the actor. "Thanks." And he hangs up.

Ten minutes later he calls back, and says, "Hi, can I speak to Sid?"

"Well, I think I just spoke to you," says the secretary, "and I told you that Sid died last week."

"Oh," says the actor.

Five minutes later the actor calls back and says, "Is Sid in?"

At this point the secretary explodes. "Look," she says angrily into the telephone, "I recognize your voice. You called twice before and I told you that Sid is DEAD! What do you keep calling for?"

"Well," says the actor, "I just love to hear you say it."

Q: What do Italians call suppositories?
A: Innuendos.

A boy is taken from his home because of physical abuse. After being in the orphanage for a few weeks, he tells a social worker that he wants to leave. The social worker asks him, "Well, do you want to go back and live with your father again?"

"No," replies the boy. "He beats me."

The social worker says, "Do you want to live with your mother?"

The boy says, "No, she beats me, too."

"Well then," asks the social worker, "who do you want to live with?"

The boy answers, "The New York Jets."

The social worker is taken aback. "The Jets? Why do you want to live with the New York Jets?"

"Because," replies the boy, "they don't beat anybody."

Q: What bird is traditionally associated with warlike tendencies and aggression?
A: The hawk.

Q: What bird is associated with peace and love?
A: The dove.

Q: What bird is traditionally associated with childbirth and the delivery of children?
A: The stork.

Q: What bird is associated with birth control?
A: The swallow.

A young couple gets married. They are real country bumpkins, and on their wedding night they don't know what to do.

The man says to the woman, "Do you know what we're supposed to do tonight?"

"No," she says, "do you?"

"No, I don't," says the man. They sit there thinking until the husband says, "Wait a minute! Down in the shipyard there are a bunch of sailors. Sailors are supposed to know about these kinds of things. I bet we could get one of them to help us out!"

So he goes down to the dock and walks up to a sailor. "Excuse me," he says, "but my wife and I just got married today and we don't know what to do. Can you help us out?"

"Sure," says the sailor. "I have a little free time. I'll be glad to do what I can."

So the two men go back to the hotel room where the wife is waiting. The sailor takes one look at the beautiful wife and immediately says to the husband, "All right, here's what you should do." He then takes out a piece of chalk, and draws a circle on the floor. He says to the groom, "Now you stand inside this circle and watch. No matter what I do, though, don't set foot outside the circle."

"Okay," says the man.

So the sailor goes over to the bed and makes love to the wife. When he's finished, he looks over at the husband standing inside the circle. The man is standing there giggling.

"What are you giggling about?" says the sailor.

The husband says, "I stepped out of the circle twice, and you didn't even notice!"

Q: Where do you find the most fish?
A: Between the head and the tail.

Two Irish women are working in the garden together, and one of them, Molly, pulls a carrot out of the ground. "Oh, my, Kathleen," she says, "this carrot really reminds me of Seamus."

"Oh, does it now?" asks Kathleen with a slight chuckle. "And what is it about this carrot that reminds you of Seamus? Is it the length, maybe?"

"No, no," says Molly, "it's not the length of it that reminds me of Seamus."

"Well, then," Kathleen inquires, flushing a bit, "is it maybe the breadth that reminds you of Seamus?"

"No," answers Molly, "it's not the breadth that reminds me of him, either."

"Good Lord," asks Kathleen, "then what exactly is it about that carrot that reminds you so much of Seamus?"

"Well," replies Molly, "it's the dirt all over it."

Q: What does a lawyer use for birth control?
A: His personality.

A very rich old man decides that when he dies he wants to take it with him. So he calls in a priest, a minister, and a rabbi and tells them, "You're the only people I can trust. I'm going to give you each a box containing a million dollars. At my funeral I want you to come up and put the three boxes into my coffin."

A couple of months later the old man dies and they have a big funeral with his body lying in state. Before the memorial service begins, the priest walks up to the casket and drops his box in. Then the minister goes up and puts his box next to the body. Finally, the rabbi goes up and places his box inside the coffin.

After the funeral, the three clergymen are together, riding away from the cemetery in a limousine. Suddenly the priest breaks out in a sweat and he starts getting all fidgety. The other two men look at him and the rabbi asks, "What's the matter with you?"

The priest says, nervously, "I can't take this. I have to confess. I took $750,000 of that money and spent it on the new church we were building and the new school we needed. I just felt it was more important to do God's work here on earth, and so I took it. But now I feel terrible about it."

"Oh, whew," gasps the minister, looking extremely relieved. "I'm really glad that you admitted that. Because, you see, I myself took out $900,000 and put it toward that new food program for the homeless that we just started. I felt just exactly the same way you did, that it was more important to do God's work here in the world."

At this point the rabbi looks aghast at the two other men. "I'm shocked," he exclaims, "shocked! Why, I put my own personal check for the *entire* amount in that coffin!"

One night I had just broken up with a girlfriend, and I was feeling a little depressed. A man about the same age as me got into my cab, and I decided to talk to him about the way I was feeling. This led to a very interesting discussion about relationships. Finally, the man said to me, "Well, there are a lot of women out there. You never know when someone will walk around the corner and it will be your next ex-lover!"

Q: Did you hear about the two gay Irishmen?
A: Gerald Fitzpatrick and Patrick Fitzgerald.

One day Donald Trump goes to a pro basketball game at Madison Square Garden. After the game he goes down to the locker room to congratulate LeBron James on being such a winner. As Trump is speaking to him, LeBron is getting dressed into his street clothes. The Donald happens to look down and notices something quite startling. "Wow," he says, "that's quite some size you have there, LeBron. That must run in the family, eh?"

"No, not at all," says LeBron. "There's a trick to it. Do you want to know what it is?"

"Are you kidding? Of course!" says Trump. "You know, small hands..."

"Well," says LeBron, who leans in close and speaks in a confidential tone, "just before you go to bed at night, you take out your thing and whack it on the bedpost three times. In no time at all you'll be surprised at how big it has gotten."

"Great!" says the Donald, and without another word, he rushes back to Trump Tower to try it out. When he gets to the bedroom all the lights are turned out, it's completely dark, and Melania is lying completely still in the bed. Trump doesn't want to wake her, but he can't wait to try out the new technique. He unzips, takes out his member, and whacks it on the bedpost three times.

Melania's voice suddenly comes out of the darkness. "LeBron, is that you?"

What do you call a person who speaks two languages?
Bilingual.
What do you call a person who speaks three languages?
Trilingual.
What do you call a person who speaks one language?
American.

A mohel (the man who performs circumcisions in a Jewish ceremony) is retiring after forty-five years of service. Throughout his career, after each circumcision, he has put the little piece of foreskin in this wallet, taken it home, and saved it.

Over the years he has collected many huge bags full of these skins, and now that he is retiring, he decides that he would like to have something made from them. He goes to the best leather designer he can find and tells him, "I would like for you to take these skins and make something out of them that will represent my career and commemorate my long service to the synagogue."

So the designer says to him, "This is a very unusual request, but I will be happy to work on such a meaningful project as this. I will use all my skills as a designer and will make something for you that will be a symbol of all your years of dedication. I am rather busy right now, but I think I can have this done for you in about three weeks."

Three weeks later the mohel returns. The leather worker is very happy to see him and, with a flourish, presents him with a small box. As the mohel opens the box, he looks somewhat crestfallen.

"A wallet?" he says. " A small wallet is all I have to show for my many years of service?"

"But, my friend," says the man, "this is no ordinary wallet! If you rub it, it becomes a suitcase!"

A woman from Germany was telling me that cab drivers in Berlin are really crazy. "In Berlin," she said, "We call a red light 'cab driver green.' We also say that the cab drivers in Berlin don't drive fast. They fly deep."

A Southern boy graduates from high school and is going north to college. Just as he is about to leave, his parents say to him, "We know you're going to be mighty lonely up there with all them Northerners, so we decided to let you take Old Blue with you. He has been our family dog for many years, and we know that Old Blue will be good company for you."

So the boy goes north with Old Blue and is only there a few weeks when he gets a call from Mary Lou, his girlfriend back home. It seems that in about eight more months they will be having a problem unless she can take care of it now, and it will cost five hundred dollars.

The boy tells Mary Lou that he will get back to her. Then he calls his folks.

"How are you?" they ask.

"Oh, I'm just fine," he says.

"And how," they ask, "is Old Blue?"

"Well, he's kind of depressed. You see, there's this woman up here who's been teaching dogs to read, and Old Blue is feeling kind of left out 'cause all the dogs can read, exceptin' him. The woman charges five hundred dollars."

"Well," says the parent, "we won't let Old Blue down. We'll send you the money."

When the boy receives the five hundred dollars a few days later, he sends it off to Mary Lou and everything is taken care of.

The boy goes home for a quick visit, and a little over a month after he gets back to school, he receives another call from Mary Lou. It seems they have the same problem again and she needs another five hundred dollars.

So the boy calls his parents and tells them that while he, himself, is fine, Old Blue is depressed again. "Old Blue has been readin' up a storm," he tells them. "He's been through all the books in the library and is now reading all the newspapers and magazines. But now the lady is teaching the dogs to talk, and Old Blue is feeling left out again. She charges five hundred dollars for talking lessons."

"We can't let Old Blue down," say the parents. "We'll send you the money."

Once again, the boy gets the money and sends it off to Mary Lou.

Then the boy is driving home in his pickup for Christmas vacation with Old Blue sitting on the seat next to him, and he just can't figure out what he is going to tell his parents. When he's in front of the Bufords' farm, the farm next to his parents', he takes his shotgun and Old Blue out of the car and shoots the dog, killing him.

When the boy reaches his parents' farm, he sees his father standing out in the driveway.

"Hello, son!" says the father. Then he looks in the pick-up and asks, "Where's Old Blue?"

"Well, Pa," says the boy, "I was driving down the road and Old Blue was reading Shakespeare and Plato and pontificating on Newton and Socrates when we passed the Bufords' farm. Old Blue said to me, 'Say, what do you think your mother would do if I told her that your father has been running over to the Bufords' farm and screwing Mrs. Buford all these years?'"

The father looks at his son and says, "You shot that dog, didn't you, boy?"

A guy goes to the doctor and his wife comes along. The doctor says to the man, "I'm going to need a urine sample, a semen sample, a blood sample, and a stool sample."

The wife says to her husband, "Why don't you just leave your underwear?"

Two sperm are swimming along after being ejaculated. They are swimming and swimming, and then one of them says to the other, "Say, do you mind if we stop and rest for a minute? I'm getting really tired."

"Sure," replies the other one. So they stop and hang out for a couple of minutes, and then they start to swim again.

A little bit later, the second sperm says, "Do you mind if we stop again? I really need to catch my breath."

"No problem," answers the first. They stop once more, and after pausing for a few minutes the two little sperms resume their journey.

After swimming for a while longer, the first sperm exclaims, "Man! I didn't know that it was such a long trip to the cervix!"

"I know!" replies the second sperm. "We haven't even passed the esophagus yet!"

Q: What do you call a drummer without a girlfriend?
A: Homeless.

A Harvard man and a Yale man are good friends, and one night, after eating dinner in a very swanky restaurant, they decide to make a quick stop in the men's room before going out to hit the town. They go into the restroom together and stand next to each other at the urinals. When they are done, the Yale man goes over to one of the sinks and rinses his hands. The Harvard man, however, just stands to the side waiting for the Yale man to finish.

As they are walking out, the Yale man says to his friend, "At Yale, they taught us to rinse our hands after we urinate."

His friend turns to him and replies, "At Harvard, they taught us not to piss on our hands."

Hitler goes to his astrologer and asks him, "When am I going to die?"

The astrologer carefully studies the astrological chart on the table in front of him, and then tells Hitler, "You will die on a Jewish holiday."

Hitler is quite surprised. "A Jewish holiday?" he asks. "How can you be so sure?"

The astrologer replies, "Any day you die will be a Jewish holiday."

A man and woman are getting undressed on their wedding night, when the bride says to the groom, "Be gentle with me, honey. I'm a virgin."

The husband is totally shocked. "How could you be a virgin?" he asks. "You've been married three times already!"

"I know," replies the bride, "but my first husband was an artist, and all he wanted to do was look at my body. My second husband was a psychiatrist, and all he wanted to do was talk about it. And my third husband was a lawyer, and he just kept saying, 'I'll get back to you next week!'"

Or the variation where the third husband was a writer: "And my third husband was a writer, and all he would do is sit on the edge of the bed, telling me how good it was going to be!"

Or the third husband was a politician: "And my third husband was a politician, and all he would do is sit on the edge of the bed, telling me all the great things he was going to do for me!"

Q: What do you call a boomerang that doesn't come back?
A: A stick.

One night in Washington, when George W. Bush was president, there was a heavy snowfall. When the president woke up in the morning, he looked out the window and saw a beautiful blanket of snow covering the White House lawn.

He was snapped out of his peaceful reverie when he noticed, written on the lawn in yellow snow, "W is an idiot."

The president got very angry and summoned the FBI and the CIA.

"I want that urine analyzed," he ordered them. "And I want to find out who the culprit is right now, *without delay!* This is *top priority!*"

Early in the afternoon a representative of the two agencies reported back to Bush. "Sir," he said, "we have tested the urine and we know whose it is. However, there is some good news and some bad news. Which would you like first?"

"Oh, no," said Bush. "I guess you had better give me the good news first."

"Well, sir," said the man, "we analyzed the urine, and it is Dick Cheney's."

"Oh, no," cried Bush, and then suddenly the realization hit him: "That's the *good* news? What could be worse than that?"

The man answered him, "It was in Laura's handwriting."

A guy goes up to a Jewish man and says, "How come you Jews always answer a question with a question?"

The Jewish man shrugs his shoulders and replies, "Why shouldn't we?"

A guy goes over to his friend's house and knocks on the door. When it opens, though, it is the friend's wife who is standing there. "Oh hi, Phyllis," says the guy, "is Gary home?"

"No, he's not, Bobby," Phyllis replies, "he won't be home from work for another twenty minutes. Would you like to come in and wait?"

Bobby thinks for a moment and then says, "Yeah, okay Thanks!"

They go in, sit down, and then suddenly Bobby blurts out, "I know I shouldn't say this, Phyllis, but you've got the most beautiful breasts in the world. As a matter of fact, I would give a hundred dollars if I could take a peek at just one of them."

Phyllis is quite taken aback, but after she recovers from her shock, she finds that she feels a little bit flattered. Then, thinking of the hundred dollars, she decides, "Oh, what the hell," and opens her bathrobe, exposing one marvelously shaped mound.

Bobby immediately pulls out a hundred dollar bill and slaps it down on the table. "That was fantastic!" he exclaims.

They sit there in silence for a few moments, then Bobby says to her, "You know, Phyllis, that was so amazing that I would give another hundred dollars to see them both together. What do you say?"

Phyllis thinks to herself, and after just a moment's hesitation, she pulls open her robe and lets the guy stare at her perfect pair. After the guy gets a nice long look, Phyllis closes up her bathrobe, and then Bobby whips out another hundred dollar bill. He plops it down on the table and says, "Incredible, just incredible!"

Bobby then gets to his feet and says, "Well, I have to get going. Thanks a lot!"

About fifteen minutes later, Gary arrives home. Phyllis says to him, "Oh, by the way, your friend Bobby dropped by."

"Oh yeah?" says Gary, a little surprised. "Well, tell me, did that jerk drop off the two hundred bucks he owes me?"

I was talking one evening to a businessman. He told me that he had been waiting in line at the bank that day when suddenly, thieves burst in and began a robbery. "The most remarkable thing about the whole incident," the man said, "was that during the entire time that the bank was being held up, no one *got out of line!"*

Q: Did you hear about the new gay Chinese restaurant?
A: The most popular dish there is Sum Yung Gai.

During World War II, an American is captured by the Germans in the African desert. The man is brought before the Nazi commander and made to stand at attention under the blazing sun.

The commander says to the American, "We do not go by the usual laws and conventions out here in the desert. What we are going to do is give you a choice. We can execute you now, or you can try to pass three tests. If you pass all three tests, you may go free."

So the American says, "Well, what are the three tests?"

The German says, "You see those three tents over there? In the first tent are five bottles of vodka. You must go into that tent and drink all five bottles, until they are completely empty.

"Then you must go into the next tent. In that tent there is a lion with an impacted tooth. You must remove that impacted tooth from the lion's mouth with your bare hands."

The American gulps, then asks, "What's in the third tent?"

"Should you pass the first two tests," says the Nazi commander, "in the third tent there is a woman who has never been sexually satisfied in her life. You must satisfy her

135

totally and completely. She must walk out of the tent with you and say, 'I have been sexually satisfied beyond my wildest dreams.'

"After you have successfully completed those three tests you may go free."

The American says to the commander, "The only other choice I have is execution, right?"

"That's right," says the German.

So the American goes into the first tent and drinks all five bottles of vodka. He then staggers out and asks to be pointed toward the second tent. The German soldiers push him in the right direction, and after a few minutes of lurching, stumbling, and zigzagging, he enters the second tent.

All of a sudden the lion lets out a tremendous roar, and the walls of the tent begin to flap violently. This continues for quite a while with much roaring and crashing coming from inside the tent. Then suddenly everything is quiet and still. A few moments later the American soldier staggers out from the tent all bloody and scratched, his uniform in tatters.

He weaves up to the Nazi commander and says drunkenly, "All right now! Where's that bitch with the impacted tooth?"

An Englishman told me this Irish joke:

Q: Why do the Irish have potatoes and the Arabs have oil?
A: The Irish got first choice.

One day a teacher tells her fourth-grade class, "Children, today we are going to start sex education. Now, the first subject I am going to discuss is *positions*. Do any of you children know any positions?"

Immediately a boy in the back of the room raises his hand and waves it frantically.

"Yes, Frankie?" she says.

The boy exclaims, "I know a *hundred* positions!"

"Ahem, well..." says the teacher a little nervously, "I don't think we have time to discuss a hundred positions right now, but if any of you children know just one or two..." She looks around the room, but none of the other children raise their hands.

"Well, I guess *I'll* start it off," says the teacher. "We'll begin by discussing the basic position, which is the woman on the bottom and man on the top."

Suddenly little Frankie starts to frantically wave his hand again.

"Yes, Frankie?" says the teacher.

"*That*," says Frankie excitedly, "makes a hundred and *one*!"

Q: Why did the Duddish grandmother have her tubes tied.
A: She didn't want any more grandchildren.

A comedian from New York returns to his hotel late one night after performing at a small comedy club in the Midwest. He steps into the elevator and just as the doors are closing, a woman in a low-cut dress quickly gets in with him. In the sexiest voice imaginable, she says to the comedian, "I just have to tell you that I think that a sense of humor is incredibly sexy! I saw you perform tonight, and you were so funny that you got me really turned on. I'm so hot for you right now that I want to take you up to your hotel room, lick you from head to toe, and then screw your brains out."

"Wow!" says the comedian. "Did you see the *first* show or the *second* show?"

I had a guy in my cab who told me that he had a friend who was a comedian. "My friend," said the guy, "was going up to Harlem to perform in a club at midnight last Saturday night. He asked me to go with him, but I said, 'Are you crazy? You're a white guy, and you're going up to Harlem

that late at night?' But he said, 'Aw, everything will be all right.' So he went up there and you know what happened?"

"He got robbed?" I asked.

The guy, in a very serious tone, said, "Somebody stole his act."

This same guy then said to me, "You know, I'm a comedy writer, too. As a matter of fact, I'm working on a joke for David Letterman. It's a great joke. I have it almost finished except for one line."

Q: How do you get a blonde to laugh on Monday?
A: Tell her a joke on Friday.

There are three big-game hunters in the jungle in Africa, a German, a Frenchman, and a guy from Brooklyn. Suddenly they are captured by cannibals and brought before the chief. The chief tells them, "By tribal custom, I am required to allow each of you a chance to escape, and I have to give you any weapon of your choice. However, I must warn you: If we catch you, we're going to skin you and make a canoe out of you." Before they even get a chance to get their breath, the chief points to the German and asks, "You're first, what do you want?"

The German says, "I want a gun."

The chief hands him a gun, and the German takes off into the jungle. Well, pretty soon the gun runs out of bullets and the natives catch up to him. They shoot him with poison darts, and within fifteen minutes they skin him and make a canoe out of him.

The other two guys see this whole thing happen, and they look at each other. "Holy cow," one of them says to the other, "what are we going to do?"

The chief points to the Frenchman. "You're next. What do you want?"

The Frenchman says, "I want a horse."

The chief looks at him and says, "Well, that's not really a weapon, but if you want a horse, I'll give you a horse."

So the Frenchman rides off into the jungle. However, he is very quickly surrounded by fifty natives on all sides, and he can't go anywhere. The natives shoot him with poison darts, skin him, and make a canoe out of him.

Finally, the chief looks at the guy from Brooklyn. "What do you want?"

The Brooklynite says, "I want a fork."

"A *fork?*" asks the chief. "What do you want a fork for?"

"Look," says the guy from Brooklyn, "you said I could have anything I wanted. Now give me the fork, all right"

"Okay, okay," says the chief. "Here's the fork."

Immediately the guy from Brooklyn takes the fork and starts stabbing himself all over. The chief stares at him and exclaims, "What are you doing?"

The guy from Brooklyn says, "Hey, Jerk!! Make a canoe out of *this!*"

Q: What's black and brown and looks good on a lawyer?
A: A Doberman.

The first manned space voyage goes to Mars. When the astronauts finally touch down on the surface of the red planet, they look around at the unusual landscape. They climb down the ladder and as soon as they set foot on the strange planet, they see an odd-looking vehicle driving right toward them. It quickly pulls up to within ten feet of where the astronauts are standing, and then stops.

The door opens and a Martian gets out. "Where are you

from?" asks the Martian, in perfect English.

One of the astronauts draws himself up to his full height and proudly says, "We're from Earth!"

"Oh, wow!" exclaims the Martian. "You're from Earth! Do you know a guy named...?"

An eighty-year-old man marries a twenty-year-old girl. A friend says to him, "Hey, can't that be fatal?"

The old man says, "If she *dies*, she *dies*."

A cab driver says to a beautiful woman in his taxi, "If I gave you some money, would you sleep with me?"

The woman angrily replies, "How dare you?"

But before she can say any more, the cabbie quickly says, "Wait a minute, lady, wait a minute! Before you get all upset, let me ask you something. If I was as handsome as a movie star, had the body of a champion athlete, was one of the wealthiest men in the world, and I offered you two million dollars to spend one night with me, then would you sleep with me?"

The woman sits back and thinks for a minute. "Well," she says, "if you were all that, then I guess I have to admit that I would."

"In that case," says the driver, "will you screw me for twenty-five bucks?"

"What?" says the indignant woman. "Just what kind of woman do you think I am?"

"We've already established that," replies the cabbie. "Now we're just dickering over price."

Just after God invented Adam, he said to his newly created man, "I have some good news for you, and some bad news. The good news is that I gave you a very large brain, and a very large penis."

Adam exclaims, "That sounds great!"

"The *bad* news," says God, "is that I only gave you enough blood to operate *one* of them at a time."

I have often wondered where jokes come from and have had many discussions about this with my passengers. One theory was that jokes are made up in prisons.

The theory that I have heard most often, though, is that stockbrokers create many of the jokes. It is true that as soon as news hits the street, jokes about it mysteriously appear, and they do seem to emanate from the Wall Street area.

One night I was discussing this question with a fare when he told me that he had indeed met one of these brokers many years ago. The broker told the man that he had created many jokes and could, in fact, make up a joke about anything at all. He challenged the man to come up with a subject and the man said, "Okay, cowboys and Indians."

The broker thought for only a moment, the man in the cab told me, then told him a joke that went on to become very popular. This man then told me the joke, and I actually had heard it many years ago. You may have heard it, too. It goes like this:

Two cowboys come upon an Indian lying on his stomach with his ear to the ground. One of the cowboys stops and says to the other, "You see that Indian?"

"Yeah," says the other cowboy.

"Look," says the first one, "He's listening to the ground. He can hear things for miles in any direction."

Just then the Indian looks up.

"Covered wagon," he says, "about two miles away. Have two horses, one brown, one white. Man, woman, child, household effects in wagon."

"Incredible!" says the cowboy to his friend. "This Indian knows how far away they are, how many horses, what color they are, who is in the wagon, and what is in the wagon. Amazing!"

The Indian looks up and says, "Ran over me about a half hour ago."

So now we know the origin of that old classic.

Q: Did you hear about the new Barbi doll, "Divorced Barbi"?
A: She comes with Ken's things, too.

A therapist says to her new patient, "So, you said that you wanted to see me because you keep obsessing about your mother. Can you tell me a little bit about that?"

"Well," says the man, "it started last week. One day I woke up and I started thinking about my mother. I couldn't get her out of my mind, so I called her to see if everything was all right. She said that she was fine, but that didn't help me. I still kept thinking about her all day and all night. Every night now, I lie awake thinking about her. I can't sleep until I go downstairs and eat a piece of dry toast."

The therapist says to him, "Just one piece of dry toast for a big boy like you?"

Q: In the Jewish faith when does the fetus become a human being?
A: When it graduates from medical school.

An older man's wife dies, and a number of years later he decides that he would like to remarry. Shortly after that, he meets a woman he likes very much, so he proposes to her.

"Before I can give you my answer," says the woman, "I must tell you a few of my needs. First of all, I must have a condominium in Florida."

"No problem," says the man. "I already have a condominium there."

"Also," she says, "I must have my own bathroom."

"You've got it," he says.

The woman then looks the man in the eye. "And sex?" she asks.

"Infrequently," replies the man.

The woman thinks for a moment, then says, "Is that one word or two?"

A drunk walks into a bar and sits down. In front of each stool he sees three darts. He calls the bartender over and says, "Hey! What are these darts here for?"

The bartender says, "Well, you take the darts and throw them at the dartboard behind the bar here, and anybody that gets three bull's-eyes in a row wins a prize."

"Oh," says the drunk, stifling a burp, "all right." He picks up a dart and, weaving from side to side, hurls it, clutching the bar at the last moment just in time to prevent himself from falling off the stool. Amazingly the dart lands firmly in the center of the bull's-eye.

He picks up the second dart, and with one hand on the bar steadying himself as best he can, he throws it. With his follow-through he collapses onto the bar, his head hitting the wood with a resounding thump. Incredibly, though, the dart lodges itself right next to the other one. Another perfect bull's-eye.

The drunk then pushes himself up off the bar, picks up the third dart, and takes careful aim with two eyes that are looking in different directions. As he throws the last dart he falls backward off the stool and lands in a heap on the floor.

But miraculously the dart lands once again in the bull's-eye.

As he stands up and wobbles over to the bar the drunk says loudly, "I want a prize! I want a prize!"

The bartender, astounded, says to him, "Okay, buddy. Okay. You'll get your prize. Just hang on a minute." As he turns around the bartender thinks to himself, "What am I going to *do*? Nobody has ever won before. What am I going to give this guy?"

Looking around the bar, he sees an old aquarium in the corner. He goes over, rolls up his sleeve, reaches into the water, and pulls out a nice, medium-size turtle. He goes back behind the bar and walks up to the drunk. "Okay, pal," he says, "here's your prize!"

The drunk's bloodshot eyes light up for an instant and he says, "Thanks a lot!" He then takes the turtle and staggers out of the bar.

A couple of weeks pass and then one day the same drunk stumbles back into the bar. He sits down at the same stool and calls out to the bartender, "I wanna try for a prize! I wanna try for a prize!"

The bartender walks over and says, "All right, buddy, go ahead."

The drunk then manages to repeat his previous performance with the one difference being that this time he manages to fall off the bar stool after every shot. However, he does make the three bull's-eyes.

"I want a prize!" he shouts. "I want a prize!" The bartender is totally flabbergasted. He says to the drunk, "I can't believe it! Nobody has ever done this before, and you've done it twice in a row!"

The drunk says, "Well, give me my -- gulp! -- p-p-prize."

The bartender says, "To tell you the truth, buddy, I just don't know what to give you. What did I give you last time?"

The drunk belches, smiles dreamily, and says, "Roast beef on a hard roll."

The Post Office stopped production on the new stamp commemorating the American lawyer. People didn't know which side to spit on.

A young guy walks into a hardware store. He goes up to the owner standing at the cash register and asks for a job.

"Well," says the owner, "at the moment I *do* happen to need somebody But tell me, can you *sell*?"

"Sure," says the young man.

"I'm not sure if you really understand me," says the owner. "I mean, can you *sell*?"

"Yep," says the guy, "I can."

The owner sees a customer coming in the door and says, "Okay, just to make sure you know what I'm talking about, watch me!"

The customer walks up and asks where the grass seed is. The owner tells him that it is in the third aisle over, the fourth shelf down. When the man comes back to the cash register with the grass seed, the owner says to him, "Do you need a lawn mower? We have a special sale on lawn mowers at the moment."

"What do I need a lawn mower for?" says the customer. "I don't even have any grass yet."

"Maybe not now," the owner replies, "but eventually you will. And then you'll need a lawn mower, and you won't be able to get one any cheaper than what we're selling them for now."

"Hmmmmm, I guess you're right," says the customer. "Okay. I'll take the lawn mower too."

After the customer leaves the owner says to the young guy, "So, do you think you can do that?"

"Sure," he says.

"Okay," says the owner, "I have to make a deposit at the

bank. I'll only be gone a few minutes, but while I'm away, watch over the store for me. And remember, if anyone comes in, *sell, sell, sell!*"

So the owner leaves, and a few minutes later a woman comes in. She goes up to the Duddish man at the cash register and asks where the tampons are.

"Fifth aisle over, second shelf down," the guy tells her.

When she comes back to pay for them, he asks her, "you wanna buy a lawn mower?"

"What would I want a lawn mower for?" she asks.

"Well," says the guy, "you're not going to be screwing around, so you might as well mow the lawn."

Q: What are a Jewish-American princess's first words?
A: Gucci, Gucci, Gucci.

Q: What's a Duddish cocktail?
A: Perrier and water.

Then there's the story of the bottomless bartender. Everyone called him Shorty, especially the women, but it wasn't because he had a short memory. It was because he had a tattoo on his penis that said, "Shorty."

What the women didn't realize, though, was that when he got excited, the tattoo said, "Shorty's Restaurant and Pizzeria...Featuring the very finest authentic Italian American cuisine...Open 24 hours, seven days a week...For free delivery, dial 522-4000...In New Jersey, dial 201...For complete menu, see other side."

But what really made it hard for him was that it was written in Braille.

Note: When verbally telling this joke, pause after saying, "Shorty's Restaurant and Pizzeria." As the laugh that you get begins to die down, add the phrase, "Featuring the finest in Italian-American cuisine." When that laugh starts to fade, say, " Open 24 hours, seven days a week." Keep adding the lines that way and the laughs will build and keep coming! (No pun intended.)

A man goes to the doctor and tells him, "Doc, I'm having a really hard time controlling my bladder."

The Doctor says, "Get off my new carpet! Right now!"

Q: What do you call a brunette walking down the street between two blondes?

A: Interpreter.

A psychiatrist decides he wants to test dogs to see if they pick up any characteristics from their owners. So he gets an architect's dog, a mathematician's dog, and a musician's dog.

First he puts the architect's dog in a room with a big pile of bones. Through a one-way window the psychiatrist carefully observes the dog's reaction. Right away the architect's dog builds a little skyscraper out of bones, then builds a couple of little houses and a little bridge. The doctor scribbles furiously, trying to write all this down.

Next he puts the mathematician's dog in the room with the pile of bones. Well, right away the mathematician's dog divides the pile into two equal halves, then divides those piles into two equal halves. The dog then takes two bones from one pile and adds them to the next pile, then takes two bones from that pile and adds them to the next one, and so on. The psychiatrist is writing like mad, unable to believe his eyes.

When the doctor is ready for the next dog, however, the musician's dog is a half hour late, eats all the bones, screws the other two dogs, then takes the rest of the day off.

A well-dressed gentleman with a slight Spanish accent got into my taxi one evening. When he told me that he was a psychiatrist, I told him that my father is a psychotherapist.

"Oh," said the man, "so you are put together well!"

I laughed and told him my father is also a minister, and he said, "Oh, so you are put together very well!"

I laughed again and said, "Well, what about you? You're a psychiatrist! You must be put together well."

"Oh, no," said the man. "Shrinks are the worst! Shrinks are held together with Scotch tape!"

Two WASPs are making love. Afterward the man says to the woman. "What's the matter? Didn't you like it?"

The woman says, "Of course I liked it. What gave you the idea that I didn't?"

"Well," says the man, "you moved."

Two retired Jewish men meet while they are vacationing in Florida. One of the men, Murray, is from Georgia and the other man, Irving, is from New York. At the end of their two week stay in the Sunshine State, Murray says to his new friend, "Irving, in these two weeks I feel like I've known you all my life. Before you go back to New York, why don't you extend your vacation for a few days and come visit me in Georgia? After all, you're retired, and there's nothing urgent calling you back home. I have a big mansion, a live-in cook, and you can come to see my town and the kind of life I lead. What do you say?"

Irving replies, "That sounds like a great idea."

The two men travel together to Georgia. They spend two days together enjoying life on the large estate. The cook provides them with wonderful meals, and Irving enjoys sleeping in the beautiful guest room with the four poster bed

151

and antique furniture.

After spending the second night in the luxurious domicile, Irving has a wonderfully cooked gourmet breakfast with his friend. After breakfast, Murray leans over a hands Irving a piece of paper.

Irving looks at the paper, and it is an itemized bill for his stay at the mansion. "Murray," he says, "what is this? It says here that you're charging me for all the food prepared for me by your chef, and that there's even a room fee for each night that I slept here. What's going on?"

"That's correct," Murray replies. "That's your bill for your stay up to now."

Irving is astounded. "You can't be serious," he implores.

Murray is unwavering. "You ate the food and slept in the room, didn't you?"

"Yes, I did," answers Irving, "but you invited me. I thought I was your guest!"

Murray says, "You are my guest, but you still have to pay."

"That's ridiculous!" exclaims Irving. "I'm not paying."

Murray says, "Why don't we go to my rabbi and let him settle this?"

"That's an excellent idea," answers Irving. "Let's go see your rabbi."

The two men go to Murray's town rabbi and Irving explains the situation to him. When Irving is finished, the rabbi says to him, "Okay. Let me see if I have this straight. Murray invited you to be a guest in his home, and then after two nights, he presented you with a bill. Is that correct?"

"That's it exactly," replies Irving.

"But," asks the rabbi, "did you actually eat the food and sleep in the bed?"

"Yes," says Irving.

The rabbi looks Irving straight in the eye and says, "Then there's no question about it. You have to pay."

Irving is dumbfounded. He and Murray walk out of the rabbi's office and get into Murray's limo. Once inside, Irving gets out his checkbook and writes out a check for the entire amount. With a scowl, he hands the check to Murray. Murray immediately takes the check and rips it up. Now Irving is completely flabbergasted. "What is going on?" he asks. "Why did you make me go through all that?"

"How else," says Murray, "could I show you what a stupid rabbi we have?"

Q: What's the difference between a vitamin and a hormone?
A: You can't make a vitamin.

One Wednesday afternoon, a fourth-grade teacher announces to her class, "Children, I'm going to ask you a question, and if anyone can answer it correctly, they can take tomorrow off from school."

Of course, this gets the immediate and undivided attention of all the students. They lean forward in their chairs and listen intently.

"All right," says the teacher, "here is the question: How many grains of sand are there on the beach at Coney Island?"

Needless to say, none of the children knows the answer.

The following day, the teacher says, "If you can answer today's question correctly, you can take tomorrow off from school. The question is: How many drops of water are there in the Hudson River?"

The children sit in silence, frustrated by this second impossibly difficult question. Dirty Ernie, sitting in the back of the class, is particularly annoyed. "I'm going to fix her," he thinks. That night, he goes home and paints two golf balls black.

Friday, the teacher says, "Okay, here is today's question..." But before she can get it out, Dirty Ernie rolls the two painted golf balls to the front of the room. With a loud clatter, the golf balls hit the wall right below the blackboard. Startled, the teacher looks around the room and says, "All right, who's the comedian with the black balls?"

"Chris Rock," Ernie replies. "I'll see ya Tuesday."

Some tourists in the Museum of Natural History are marveling at the dinosaur bones. One of them asks the guard, "Can you tell me how old the dinosaur bones are?"

The guard replies, "They are three million, four and a half years old."

"That's an awfully exact number," says the tourist. "How do you know their age so precisely?"

The guard answers, "Well, the dinosaur bones were three million years old when I started working here, and that was four and a half years ago."

A man comes home and finds his partner in bed with his wife. "Max!" he exclaims. "I *have* to. But *you*...?"

Three guys are talking about bars in their respective hometowns. The first guy, an Irish man, proudly boasts, "Up in Boston, we've got this place called 'Paddy's.' If you go into Paddy's and buy your first drink, then buy a second, Paddy will give you the third drink on the house!"

The next guy, an Italian from New York, says, "Well, in Brooklyn we've got this place called 'Vinnie's.' Now, if you go into Vinnie's and buy two or three drinks, Vinnie will let you drink the rest of the night for free!"

The third guy, a Duddish man, says, "Well, in Chicago, we've got this place called Bob's. When you go into Bob's, you get your first drink for free, your second drink free, your third drink free, and then a bunch of guys take you into the back room and get you laid. All for free!"

"Wow!" says the Irish guy. "That's really remarkable!"

The guy from New York says, "Yeah! That's incredible! Did that actually happen to you?"

"Well," replies the Duddish guy, "it didn't happen to me personally, but it happened to my sister!

Q: What did the Deadhead say when he stopped taking acid and ran out of weed?
A: "This music *sucks!*"

Q: How many Deadheads does it take to change a light bulb?
A: None. They just wait till it burns out and then follow it around all over the country.

Q: Why do Deadheads wave their hands in front of their faces during concerts?
A: To keep the music out of their eyes.

It is Ronald Reagan's second term in the presidency, and Washington is suddenly infested with rats. No one can explain why it has happened, but it has quickly become a serious problem. The government officials try everything, but nothing seems to get rid of the rodents. In desperation the government officials place an ad for anyone knowing of any means to rid the city of this terrible nuisance.

One day a little man in a green suit shows up at the gate of the White House and asks to see the president. He is about to be turned away when he says that he has come in response to the advertisement. He is taken immediately to see President Reagan.

"I can get rid of your rat problem in a number of hours," says the little man in a strange, unfamiliar foreign accent. "It will only cost you five hundred dollars."

"All right," says the president, "that sounds reasonable. You've got the job."

The little man then reaches into a sack he is carrying over his shoulder and pulls out a little bright green rat. He puts the rat down on the floor and walks out the door.

The rat follows him, and as the man walks through the city, all the rats fall in behind. They come from everywhere, and soon there is a huge horde of rats swarming through the city behind the little man in the green suit and his little green rat.

The man walks down to the Potomac, and the little green rat jumps in. All the other rats follow and are instantly drowned in the river, ridding Washington of its rodent problem.

President Reagan happily goes up to the little man and hands him five hundred dollars.

But the man refuses to take the money. "No, no," he says, "I have decided that this will just be a favor I have done for the president of the United States. Good day." And with that he starts to turn and walk away.

"Uh, just a moment, little fellow," says Reagan.

"Yes?" replies the man.

Reagan sidles up to the man and says to him in a low voice, "Do you, by any chance, have any little green Democrats?"

A Duddish airliner comes in for a landing at LaGuardia Airport. As it approaches the runway, the pilot gets really scared that he's not going to make it, so he quickly reverses the thrust on the jet engines and as soon as the wheels touch the landing strip, he jams on the breaks. The plane comes to a screeching halt.

"Whew!" he gasps to the co-pilot, who is picking up his hat. "That was so close, I wasn't sure if we were going to make it! That has got to be the shortest runway I've ever seen in my life!"

"Yeah!" exclaims the co-pilot. "And did you also notice how wide it is?"

A lady wants a few rooms painted in her house. She sees some men across the street doing some yard work. She calls out to them and asks to see the foreman. He says that he'll be right over. A few minutes later the man leaves his crew of workers, and knocks on her door.

The lady opens the door and asks, "Do you ever do painting jobs?"

The foreman says, "Yes, we do."

"I'll show you what I need to have done." The lady takes him into the living room and sayx, "First of all, I would like this room to be painted white."

"All right," says the man. He goes over to the window, opens it up, and calls out to the workers across the street, "Green side up!"

Next she takes him upstairs to her bedroom and says, "I think this room would look good in a nice shade of beige."

The man walks over to the window and calls out "Green side up!"

Then the woman takes him into the bathroom and says, "I think light blue would be a good color in here."

Once again the man yells out the window, "Green side up!"

"Wait a minute," says the woman, "I don't understand. I thought for a minute that maybe you had a code here or something. But how come one room is white, one room is beige, another one is blue, and they're all 'green side up'?"

"Oh, no, lady," says the man. "That has nothing to do with your rooms. It's just that I have some Duddish guys across the street laying sod."

One night while I was driving my cab I was in an accident. I was taken to the hospital and was pronounced clinically dead for five minutes before I was revived. During the time I was "dead," I went to heaven, and I clearly remember what it was like. I was walking around checking out everything, and I saw a large wall with hundreds of clocks on it. But, oddly, the clocks had only minute hands, and they would jump at irregular intervals. An angel happened to be passing by, and I asked her what these clocks were for.

"Oh," she said, "that's how we keep track of how often people masturbate on earth."

I looked more closely, and sure enough, under each clock there was a little nameplate. So I had a marvelous time looking up all the people I knew. But after a few minutes I said to the angel, "Wait a minute, I don't see my best friend Jeremy Johnson's name here."

The angel said, "Oh, yes. They keep that one over in the office. They're using it for a fan."

Q: What do you have when you have one lawyer in a town?
A: Too little work.

Q: What do you have when you have two lawyers in a town?
A: Too much work.

After dropping off some people at Tavern on the Green during the height of the Christmas season, I was about to pull out onto Central Park West, when a man and woman approached my cab. The woman tapped on my window so I rolled it down.

"Do you know," she asked, "where I can find the exposition with the three wise guys?"

I managed to choke back my laughter long enough to tell them that I didn't know where it was, and I was able to drive off before giving in to the temptation of saying to her, "You mean Moe, Larry, and Curly?"

A Jewish man, a Duddish man, and a man from India are driving around looking for a hotel. Unfortunately a convention happens to be in town that night, and there are no rooms available.

They wind up driving to the outskirts of the city where at last they come across a motel with a VACANCY sign. They stop and go in to register.

"I'm sorry," says the clerk, "but we only have one room left and it's only a double."

The three men explain how desperate they are, and so the clerk says, "Okay. I know what we can do. One of you men can sleep out in the barn. Don't worry, though, we'll put a cot out there and make it nice and comfortable for you."

The clerk then shows them to their room, and as he is leaving he says, "It's just up to you three to decide who is going to sleep in the barn."

Without hesitation the man from India says, "No problem. I'll sleep in the barn."

He leaves, and a few minutes later, as the other two men are getting ready for bed, they hear a knock on the door. They open it, and the Indian man is standing there. "So sorry," he says, "I cannot sleep with the sacred cow."

"So I'll sleep in the barn," says the Jewish man and he leaves. A few minutes later the other two men hear a knock on the door. They answer it, and the Jewish guy is standing there. He shrugs and says, "Can't sleep with the pig."

So the Duddish guy says, "I guess I'll sleep in the barn."

He leaves. The Indian and the Jewish man are beginning to undress when they hear a sound at the door. They open it and the pig and the cow are standing there.

Q: What has four legs, is big, green, furry, and if it fell out of a tree it would kill you?
A: A pool table.

Two law partners hire a new cute young secretary and a contest arises between them as to who can bed her first, even though they're both already married. Eventually one of them scores with her and his partner is quite eager to hear how things went. "So what did you think?" asks the partner.

"Aah," replies the first lawyer, "my wife is better."

Some time goes by and then the second lawyer goes to bed with the secretary. "So," asks the first guy, "what did you think?"

"The second guy replies, "You're right."

An old rabbi is talking with one of his friends and says with a warm smile, "I gladdened seven hearts today."

"Seven hearts?" asks the friend, "how did you do that?"

The rabbi strokes his beard and replies, "I performed three marriages."

The friend looks at him quizzically. "Seven?" he asks. "I could understand SIX, but... "

"What do you think?" says the rabbi. "That I do this for free?"

Q: What's the difference between Heaven and Hell?
A: *In Heaven:*
       the policemen are English
       the cooks are French
       the mechanics are German
       the lovers are Italian
       and the whole thing is run by the Swiss

In Hell:
       the policemen are German
       the cooks are English
       the mechanics are French
       the lovers are Swiss
       and the whole thing is run by the Italians

A guy goes into the doctor and tells him that he keeps having these loud farts that don't smell. "They're really gigantic, Doc," the man says, "and it's really embarrassing. I mean, sometimes I'll be making love to a woman and suddenly out of nowhere, I'll let out this humongous fart. Fortunately, as I said, they don't smell, but they're just so loud that I'm totally mortified."

"Does this happen any other times besides lovemaking?" asks the doctor.

"Oh, sure." says the guy. "It can happen any time. I can pick up a date and be driving in my car with her when, suddenly, without any warning, this huge, loud fart will erupt and the woman will be totally shocked and I'll be completely embarrassed. As I said though, at least they don't smell. But it can happen anytime anywhere--in a restaurant during a romantic dinner, in a movie theater right at the quietest moment of the film...they just blast out. They're so loud., Doc, you gotta help me!"

"Now calm down," says the doctor, "let's take this one step at a time. First of all, I want to examine you. Turn around, drop your drawers, and bend over."

The guy does this, and as the doctor leans in to begin the examination on the man's exposed butt, all of a sudden there is this loud gigantic BOOM! that rattles the walls of the office.

"Okay," says the doctor, leaning back and straightening his hair. "I can see right away that you're going to need an operation."

The guy looks around and says, "Oh no, you mean I'm going to need an operation on my rear end?"

"No," says the doctor, "on your nose."

One night in my taxi a woman and I were talking about jokes and humor in general when she said, "My mother told me that I am a clown, as opposed to a comedian. When I asked her what the difference was, my mother said, 'People laugh with a comedian. They laugh at a clown.' I said, 'Gee, thanks, Mom.'"

A barber opens up a new shop in a small town. The first day he is open, a minister comes in. When the haircut is finished, the minister asks the barber how much he owes him. "Oh," replies the barber, "I never charge a man who does God's work."

The next morning when the barber arrives at his shop, he finds three loaves of freshly baked bread on the doorstep, with a kind note of thanks from the minister. Later that day, a priest comes into the shop. The barber gives the priest a nice haircut and when it's done, the priest inquires as to the amount of the bill. The barber tells him, "I never charge a man of the cloth."

The next morning, the barber finds three bottles of wine on the doorstep with a nice note from the priest. Near the end of the day, a rabbi comes into his barber shop. The barber gives him a haircut and when he's done, the rabbi asks, "So, how much do I owe you?"

The barber bows politely and says, "I never charge a man who works for the Lord."

The following morning, on his front doorstep, the barber finds three rabbis.

Q: What does an accountant do when he is constipated?
A: Works it out with a pencil.

A second-grade teacher says to her class, "Children, we are going to begin to study sex education. Tonight your first assignment will be to go home and find out what a penis is."

Little Freddie goes home and asks his father, "Daddy, what is a penis?"

The father pulls down his pants and points proudly, saying, "Son, *that* is a perfect penis."

The next day when the boy arrives at school, his best friend rushes up to him on the playground.

"Freddie! I forgot to find out what a penis is! What's a penis?"

Freddie says, "Come on."

So they both go into the boy's room, and Freddie pulls down his pants. He points down and says, "There; if that was a little smaller, it would be a *perfect* penis."

A little boy and a little girl are playing. The little boy pulls down his shorts and says, "*I* have one of these and you *don't*." The little girl starts crying and crying and runs home to her mother.

The next day the boy and girl are playing together again. Once again the boy points to his private parts and says, "*I* have one of these and you *don't*." But the little girl just keeps on playing. "How come," says the boy, "you're not *crying* today?"

"My mother told me that when I get older," says the little, pulling up her dress, "with one of *these* I can get as many of *those* as I want."

There are two great horn players who have been lifelong friends. They hang out together and play together for years. They are virtually inseparable. Unfortunately one of them gets hit by a truck and killed. About a week later his friend wakes up in the middle of the night with a start because he can feel a presence in the room. He calls out, "Who's there? Who's there? What's going on?"

He hears a faraway voice say, "It's me -- Bob."

Excitedly he sits up in bed.

"Bob! Bob! Is that you? Where are you?"

"Well," says the faraway voice, "I live in heaven now."

"You do? You live in heaven! Oh, my gosh! What's it like?"

"Well," says Bob, "I gotta tell you, I'm jamming up here every day. I'm playing with Bird, 'Trane, Miles, Hendrix, Jaco...and B.B. just got in. *All* the cats are here! Man, it is *smoking*!"

"Oh, wow!" says his friend. "that sounds fantastic! Tell me more, tell me more!"

"Let me put it this way," says the voice, "There's good news and there's bad news. The *good* news is that these guys

167

are in *top form*. I mean, I have *never* heard them sounding better. They are *wailing* up here.

"The *bad* news is that God has this girlfriend who sings…"

Q: How do you make God laugh?
A: Tell him your plans.

A young man walks into a drugstore and goes up to the counter. "I'd like a dozen condoms," he proudly announces to the pharmacist. "I've been going out with this really hot babe. We've fooled around a lot, but we haven't actually gone all the way yet. But I think that tonight is going to be the night. I've got her really hot for me now." With that, the young man pays the druggist, and swaggers out of the store.

That night, the young man arrives at his girlfriend's house to take her out. She meets him outside on the front porch and says, "Since you've never met my parents, they invited you to come in and have dinner with us. After dinner we can tell them that we're going to the movies or something, so that we can get off to spend some time alone." She gives him a wink, and leads him into the house.

The family is already seated at the dinner table, and after the introductions are made, they sit down. The young man says to the family, "Would you mind if I say grace tonight?"

The mother says, "Why, I think that would be a lovely idea."

They all bow their heads, and the young man prays, "Dear Lord, we ask that you bless this food, and that you may always keep us aware of the spirit of forgiveness that was so important in the teachings of Christ. Let us always remember His words, 'To err is human, but to forgive is divine.' In Jesus' name we pray, Amen."

"That was very nice," says the mother, and the family

begins to eat. The girl leans over to the young man and whispers, "You didn't tell me that you're so religious."

The young man whispers back to her, "You didn't tell me that your father is a pharmacist."

Q: How can you tell when a lawyer is lying?
A: His lips are moving.

Two Duddish men rent a rowboat and go fishing in a lake. They are catching fish after fish, and have almost two dozen by the end of the afternoon. One man says to the other, "Why don't we come back to this same spot tomorrow?"

"Good idea," his friend answers.

So the first man takes a piece of chalk, and draws an X on the bottom of the boat.

"Don't be stupid!" the friend says. "How do you know that we'll get the same boat tomorrow?"

Q: What's the difference between a savings bond and a man?
A: A savings bond matures.

And the show biz variation:

Q: What's the difference between a savings bond and a musician?
A: Eventually, a savings bond matures *and makes money.*

169

Very late one night, I picked up a man outside the Plaza hotel. When I asked him what kind of work he did, he told me that he was the bartender there. He told me that one night many years ago, Jackie Gleason had come into the hotel bar with a number of friends. Early in the evening, Mr. Gleason said to this bartender, "So tell me, what's the biggest tip you ever got?"

The bartender replied, "A hundred dollars, Mr. Gleason."

"Well tonight," Jackie said, "I'm going to give you a hundred and fifty."

Many hours later, when Gleason was settling up his bill, he walked over to the bartender and, true to his word, gave him a hundred and fifty dollar tip. "So tell me," Jackie said, feeling pretty self-satisfied after he had handed the huge tip to the bartender, "who was it that gave you the hundred dollar tip?"

The bartender replied, "It was you, Mr. Gleason."

Jackie just threw his head back and laughed.

Three inmates from the asylum are up for review to be released. When the first one comes before the board, a member of the panel asks him, "Do you think that you're well enough to be released?"

"Yes, I do," replies the inmate.

The board member then says to him, "All right, answer this question for me. How much is three times three?"

The inmate sinks deep into thought, but suddenly brightens. "I know!" he exclaims. "Three times three is Tuesday!"

The panel members look at each other and roll their eyes as the man is ushered out of the office and back to his room. A few minutes later, the next inmate is brought in. The head of the panel asks him, "Do you think that you are now ready to leave the institution?"

"Oh yes," answers the inmate."

So the panel member says to him, "Well then, what is three times three?"

The man thinks for just a moment, and then declares triumphantly, "One hundred eighty one!"

After he is lead out, the third inmate is brought before the board. The panel member asks him, "Do you feel that you are ready to cope with the outside world?"

The inmate is very sure of himself as he answers, "Yes, I most certainly am!"

The board member then says, "Very good. Now tell me, what is three times three?"

Without a moment's hesitation, the inmate replies, "Nine."

"Very good!" exclaims the head of the review committee. "How did you arrive at that number?"

"It was simple," replies the inmate. "All I had to do was subtract Tuesday from 181."

A Duddish man said to me, "You know, you Americans have Duddish jokes, but we in Duddland tell American jokes. Would you like to hear an American joke from Duddland?"

"Sure," I said.

"Okay," said the Duddish guy. "How many Americans does it take to change a light bulb?"

I said, "I don't know. How many?"

The Duddish man said, "One."

A Jewish man boards a commercial airliner, and when he gets to his assigned seat, he finds that he has been put right next to two Arabs. The Jewish man has the aisle seat, and the Arabs are sitting in the two inside seats. The Jewish man greets the Arabs amiably, sits down, immediately takes off his shoes, and puts his feet up. He has just gotten comfortable and is about to drift off to sleep, when the Arab next to the window stands up.

"Excuse me," says the Arab, "but I'd like to go and get myself a Coke."

The Jewish man sits up and replies, "Hey, I'd be glad to get you a Coke. Just sit back down, relax, and I'll have your Coke for you in a minute."

He stands up and walks down the aisle to get the soda. While he is away, the Arab looks down and notices that the Jewish man has left his shoes on the floor. The Arab leans over and spits into one of the shoes.

A moment later the Jewish man returns. "Here is your Coke," he says kindly, handing it to the Arab. "I hope that you enjoy it."

The Jewish man sits down, puts his feet up, and has just gotten comfortable again when the Arab in the middle stands up. "Excuse me,' says the second Arab, "but that Coke looked so good that I just have to get one for myself."

"Hey," says the Jewish guy, "I'll be glad to get one for you, too. Sit there, relax, and I'll be right back." With a smile, he goes off to get the other Arab his Coke.

This time, the second Arab leans down and spits into the man's other shoe. When the Jewish man returns, he gives the second Arab his Coke. "There you go," he says, "and if you want another, please feel free to ask."

So the Jewish man finally gets to sit down and get comfortable. He puts his feet up and falls contentedly asleep.

A couple hours later, the airplane lands, and the three men start getting ready to deplane. The Jewish man puts on his shoes, and as soon as he stands up, he realizes exactly what has happened. He turns to the two Arabs next to him, and in a very exasperated voice says to them, "Oh, my God, when is all this nonsense between us going to end? The spitting in the shoes...the pissing in the Cokes..."

On the most enjoyable trip to La Guardia Airport that I ever had, one of two very nice Midwestern women told me this joke:

Q: Why was the rubber flying through the air?
A: It got pissed off.

One morning, a mother goes into her son's room and says to him, "It's time to get up! It's the first day of the new school year!"

The son scrunches down and pulls the covers up over his head. "I'm not going!" he shouts.

"Why, son," says the mother, "why don't you want to go to school?"

The son answers, "Because all the teachers hate me and

all the kids hate me."

"Son," the mother says, "it doesn't matter if the teachers hate you. It doesn't matter if the kids hate you. You have to go to school today because everyone is counting on you. You're the principal!"

Rene Descartes walks into a bar and sits down. The bartender walks over to him and asks, "Would you like a drink?"

Descartes replies, "I think not," and disappears.

Jesus is out on the golf course playing a few holes with St. Peter as his caddy. As he's about to make a drive Jesus turns to St. Peter and asks, "Which club do you think I should use for this shot?"

St. Peter looks over the course and says, "The seven iron."

"I don't know," says Jesus. "I think Tiger Woods would use the nine."

St. Peter shakes his head. "I think you'd better use the seven iron, Jesus. Look, you have the sand trap in front of the green, and the lake beyond."

"Nah," says Jesus. "I think Tiger Woods would use the nine. Give me the nine."

So St. Peter hands Jesus the nine iron, and Jesus hits the ball. It goes sailing out, bounces once on the green, and then splashes into the lake.

They go walking down to the lake, and, of course, Jesus walks across the water to fetch his ball.

A fellow happens to pass by, sees Jesus walking on the water, and says to St. Peter, "Who does that guy think he is, Jesus Christ?"

"Naaah," says St. Peter. "He thinks he's Tiger Woods."

Q: What's the difference between boogers and broccoli?
A: Kids won't eat broccoli.

A little boy goes up to the counter in a drugstore and asks the clerk for a box of Tampax. The clerk puts them into a paper bag and says to the boy, "Are these for your mommy?"

"No," says the boy.

"Well, then," says the clerk, "are they for your sister?"

"Uh-uh," says the boy.

"Well, then," says the clerk, "who are they for?"

"They're for me," says the boy.

"For you?" says the surprised clerk. "What are you going to do with them?"

"I don't know yet," says the boy. "All I know is that I keep seeing on TV that if you buy these, you can go horseback riding, swimming, camping ..."

Q: What's the difference between capitalism and communism?
A: Under capitalism, man exploits man, whereas under communism, it's the other way around.

A young boy needs to go the bathroom, but he'll only do it with his grandmother. He can't go by himself. So he says to his father, "Daddy, I have to go pee. Can you go get Grandma?"

The father says, "That's all right. Don't bother your Grandma. I'll take you to the bathroom."

"No, no," says the boy. "I want my grandmother."

"Why," says the father, "must you always go to the bathroom with your grandmother?"

The boy replies, "Because her hand shakes."

Years later the grandmother goes to the doctor and says, "Doctor, I'm losing my sex urge."

The doctor says, "Madam, you're ninety-three years old. You should be glad you even have a sex urge."

"I understand," says the woman, "but I still want more of a sex drive."

"All right," he says, "when did you first start noticing this?"

She says, "Last night and then again this morning."

The doctor says, "Your problem isn't that you're losing your sex urge, your problem is that you're not having enough sex. You should be having sex fifteen times a month."

So she goes home to her husband and says, "Honey, guess what? The doctor says I should be having sex fifteen times a month."

The husband says, "Okay. Put me down for three."

The ninety-six year old man's ninety-three year old wife dies. At the funeral her husband is very upset. His friend comes over to comfort him. The old man says, "She was a wonderful woman. But, above all, she was a fabulous lover, and I'll never find another like her."

His friend says, "Listen, you're a strong, vital man. You're gonna find another woman and start all over again."

"I know," says the old man, "but what am I gonna do *tonight*?"

His friend says, "Why don't you go to a house of ill repute?"

176

So, the old man goes to a brothel, knocks on the door, and the madam answers. "Can I help you?" she says.

The man says, "Yes. I'd like a woman for the night."

The madam says, "How *old* are you?"

He says, "I am ninety-six years old."

She says, "Ninety-six years old? You've had it."

"I have?" says the old man. "How much do I owe you?"

Anyway, he walks inside and says, "So, tell me something. How much is this going to cost me?"

The madam says, "Well, you're ninety-six years old. That'll be ninety-six dollars."

The man says, "You're putting me on!"

She says, "That'll be another ten dollars."

So he goes upstairs with a nice young lady, and he says to her, "Tell me, do you know how to do it the Jewish way?"

She says, "No."

He says, "Well, then, forget it."

"Wait a minute," the girl says. "I'm new at this game and I'm eager to please. You show me how to do it the Jewish way and I'll give it to you for half price."

He says, "That's *it!*"

Two weeks later he develops a urinary problem, so he goes to the doctor. He says, "Doc, I can't urinate."

The doctor says, "You're ninety-six years old. You've urinated enough."

"But, wait," says the old man, "Look, I have a discharge."

So the doctor examines the man's penis. He then asks. "When did you last have sex?"

"A week ago," says the man.

"Well, that's what it is," says the doctor. "You're coming."

The doctor then says, "How are your bowel movements?"

The man says, "I move my bowels every morning at eight o'clock."

"That's great," says the doctor.

"No, it's not," says the old man. "I don't get out of bed until ten."

As a result of this, he goes into an old-age home.

After two weeks of consistently defecating in his bed, the nurse says to him, "If you do that one more time, you're cleaning it up yourself."

The next morning he does it again. The nurse walks in, takes one look, and says, "That's it! You clean it up!" and walks out the door.

So the man pulls the sheets from his bed and disgustedly throws them out the window. They happen to land on a drunk walking on the street below.

The drunk wildly wrestles the sheets off his head, runs into the nearest bar, and says, "Give me a double martini— quick!"

The bartender says, "Hey, buddy, what happened to you?"

"You're not going to believe this," says the drunk, "but I just beat the *crap* out of a ghost!"

A cab driver is driving down the street when suddenly he looks over and sees the pope frantically waving his arms and yelling, "TAXI! TAXI!" The cab driver immediately swerves over to the curb and the pope quickly jumps into the back seat.

"Take me to Kennedy Airport!" he cries. "My limo just broke down and I don't have time to wait for them to fix it! I just HAVE to make that last flight to Rome! Hurry!"

"You got it!" replies the cab driver. He hits the gas and they head uptown on Madison Avenue. Unfortunately, they run into a bit of traffic and have to stop for several red lights.

While they are waiting for the fourth red light to change to green, the pope is getting more and more anxious. "Hurry! Hurry!" he pleads. "I've just got to make this plane!"

"Look, your pontiffship," replies the cabbie, "This is rush hour and we've run into some traffic. I'm going as fast as I can. If I run a red light, I'll get a ticket. There's nothing more that I can do!"

At the next light, the pope becomes extremely agitated. Suddenly he gets an idea. "I'll make you a deal," he says to the cabbie, "let ME drive!"

"YOU want to drive?" asks the incredulous cab driver.

"PLEASE!" replies the pope. "This is the last flight and I can't miss it! You've got to let me drive!"

"How can I say 'no' to you?" says the cabbie. He jumps out and gets into the back seat while the pope gets out and slides into the front. As soon as he gets behind the wheel, it is 'pedal to the metal' time. With a loud screeching of tires, the pope swiftly pulls out.He begins screaming sixty miles an hour through the city streets, dodging through traffic, running red lights, and driving up on the sidewalks. He gets on the Grand Central Parkway, and when he hits ninety miles an hour a cop sees the cab fly by.

With the siren blaring and his lights flashing, the cop chases the cab for five miles before the pope finally pulls over. The police car pulls up behind the stopped cab and the cop jumps out. He walks quickly up to the driver's side of the cab and the pope rolls down the window. The policeman looks in and sees him, then nervously says, "Wait right here. Don't go away. I'll be right back!"

He runs back to the squad car and calls his sergeant. "Sarge," he says, "I just pulled this guy over, and I'm not sure whether I should give him a ticket or not. I think he's REALLY important."

"Who is it?" asks the sergeant over the radio. "Is it the mayor?"

"No," says the cop, "I think he might be more important than that."

"Is it the governor?" the sergeant asks.

"No," replies the policeman. "I think he might be more important than that."

"Did you pull over the PRESIDENT?" asks the sergeant.

"No," answers the cop, "but I think this guy might even be more important than THAT!"

"Well," says the sergeant impatiently, "who is it?"

"I don't know," replies the policeman, "but, the POPE is HIS DRIVER!"

It's really nice to have a joke where the cab driver is the big shot!

Cabbies, after all, do deserve a lot of respect for doing a tough job. It's very grueling to sit for twelve hours with virtually no breaks, fight all the traffic, and to risk the danger of accidents and robberies.

That's why I'll be eternally grateful to all of you out there who got into my cab and lightened my load with laughter.

**Remember to join me at
jimsjokezone on Facebook,
on YouTube at: Jim's Joke Zone,
and at jimsjokezone.com,
where we can share all the
LATEST LAUGHS!**

Made in United States
North Haven, CT
19 January 2024

47675585R00118